I0815953

IN THE AMERICAN WEST

ANDY WILKINSON, SERIES EDITOR

ALSO IN THIS SERIES:

Bad Smoke, Good Smoke: A Rancher's View of Texas Wildfire
by John R. Erickson
Cowboy's Lament: A Life on the Open Range
by Frank Maynard; edited by Jim Hoy
The Hell-Bound Train: A Cowboy Songbook, Second Edition
by Glenn Ohrlin; edited by Charlie Seemann
If I Was a Highway
by Michael Ventura
In My Father's House: A Memoir of Polygamy
by Dorothy Allred Solomon
Llano Estacado: An Island in the Sky
Stephen Bogener and William Tydeman, editors
Light in the Trees
by Gail Folkins
On Becoming Apache
by Harry Mithlo and Conger Beasley Jr.
Rightful Place
by Amy Hale Auker
A Sweet Separate Intimacy: Women Writers of the American Frontier, 1800–1922
Susan Cummins Miller, editor
Texas Dance Halls: A Two-Step Circuit
by Gail Folkins and J. Marcus Weekley
Texas Red
by Red Steagall, with Jim Jennings

SMALL TOWN AUTHOR

JOHN R. ERICKSON

TEXAS TECH UNIVERSITY PRESS

This book is typeset in Adobe Caslon Pro. The paper used in this book meets the minimum requirements of ANSI/NISO Z39.48-1992 (R1997). ♾

Designed by Hannah Gaskamp
Cover design by Hannah Gaskamp

Library of Congress Cataloging-in-Publication Data

Names: Erickson, John R., 1943– author. Title: Small Town Author / John R. Erickson. Description: Lubbock, Texas: Texas Tech University Press, 2025. | Series: Voice in the American West | Includes bibliographical references and index. | Summary: "A memoir spanning more than fifty years by the West Texas author best known for the Hank the Cowdog series"—Provided by publisher.
Identifiers: LCCN 2024060308 (print) | LCCN 2024060309 (ebook) | ISBN 978-1-68283-254-7 (cloth) | ISBN 978-1-68283-255-4 (ebook)
Subjects: LCSH: Erickson, John R., 1943– | Authors, American—20th century—Biography. | LCGFT: Autobiographies.
Classification: LCC PS3555.R428 Z46 2025 (print) | LCC PS3555.R428 (ebook) | DDC 813/.54 [B]—dc23/eng/20241220
LC record available at https://lccn.loc.gov/2024060308
LC ebook record available at https://lccn.loc.gov/2024060309

Texas Tech University Press
Box 41037
Lubbock, Texas 79409-1037 USA
800.832.4042
ttup@ttu.edu
www.ttupress.org

I hope this book will honor the memory of my parents, the authors who lighted my path, and the people in my hometown who helped raise me.

CONTENTS

PREFACE / IX

PART 1: THE UNIVERSITY YEARS

CHAPTER 1: Denver and UT / 5
CHAPTER 2: The Dance / 25
CHAPTER 3: The Tower / 33
CHAPTER 4: Harvard / 37
CHAPTER 5: Boston 1967–68 / 49
CHAPTER 6: Back to Texas / 61

PART 2: THE CIVIL RIGHTS MOVEMENT

CHAPTER 7: Mississippi and New York / 69
CHAPTER 8: Austin and St. Johns / 83

PART 3: BACK TO THE PRAIRIE

CHAPTER 9: Joe and Anna Beth / 97
CHAPTER 10: Farmhand / 109
CHAPTER 11: The Country Club / 117

CHAPTER 12: Character Sketches / **125**
CHAPTER 13: Border Town / **137**

PART 4: WRITERS AND WRITING

CHAPTER 14: Reading and Study / **145**
CHAPTER 15: Al Dewlen and Foster-Harris / **151**
CHAPTER 16: Haley and Goodnight / **157**
CHAPTER 17: Andy Wilkinson: History, Poetry, and Song / **167**
CHAPTER 18: John Graves / **171**
CHAPTER 19: Herman Wouk / **181**
CHAPTER 20: Marc Simmons and Larry McMurtry / **189**
CHAPTER 21: Western Writers / **199**
CHAPTER 22: Elmer Kelton / **205**

PART 5: FINDING A VOICE

CHAPTER 23: The Cowboy Years / **215**
CHAPTER 24: Back to Perryton / **221**
CHAPTER 25: More Than a Horse Story / **227**
CHAPTER 26: Casey the Bronc / **233**
CHAPTER 27: Dead End / **241**
CHAPTER 28: Village Handyman / **245**
CHAPTER 29: Maverick Books / **253**
CHAPTER 30: Finding Hank / **265**

REFERENCES / **275**

INDEX / **277**

PREFACE

More than fifty years ago, I took what we might call Vows of Discipline and imposed upon myself a rather monkish existence: every morning, I go to my writing place and remain there for at least four hours. I can either write or not write, but I'm happier and easier to get along with when I have put words on a page.

I can't write Hank the Cowdog books all the time, so there have been days and months when I ended up writing about other things. I've written about prairie fires, Panhandle archaeology, my work as a cowboy, and a book about my mother's ranching family in West Texas (*Prairie Gothic*). *Story Craft* allowed me to ruminate on faith, culture, and writing.

In 2019, Maverick Books brought out a large-format book, *Finding Hank*, in which I addressed the most often asked questions about the character that has brought me a little dab of fame. I discussed my growing-up years in Perryton, something young readers are curious about, but didn't say much about my years of apprenticeship when I was learning my craft. *Finding Hank* was autobiographical, but the primary focus was on Hank, not me.

The present book is more about me, the author, than about Hank, the star. It begins where *Finding Hank* left off, with young John Erickson going off to college and trying to find his place in the big wide world. It covers the years from 1962 to 1983 and includes the six years I spent in university settings.

Acquiring a college education might have been a necessary step for me. I've always been a slow reader, and without the discipline of an academic institution I might never have read Plato, Shakespeare, Kant, or Dostoyevsky, but I've never felt nostalgic about those years and have written almost nothing about my college experience. I've even wondered if I might have used my time better doing something else. I was like a coyote in a cage, pacing the cell and gazing through the wire at the prairie beyond.

Part of the problem was the times. During the decade of the sixties, the entire country was dealing with wrenching social problems, an unpopular war, and unprecedented change. When I look back at the young man who was me during the hurricane years of the sixties, living in Denver, Austin, Cambridge, and New York, parts of the story still don't make sense, even with the benefit of hindsight.

Another problem is that my life has involved a series of abrupt changes, as though I left a room, closed the door, and never went back: from big city to small town; from social activist to flunky bartender; from church work to ranch work; from aspirations of being a Man of Literature to publishing my own books. It was all part of the same story, but it seems . . . well, untidy, disorganized. Life. It doesn't exactly fit together.

When I was beginning to think about the possibility of becoming a writer, I wasn't aware of any precedent for a Texas author moving back to his hometown and writing for the people in that region. We might even say that the education systems in small towns encouraged talented students to do the opposite, to leave home and prove themselves in a bigger, brighter place. Finding a good job and buying a house in suburban Dallas or Houston were markers of success.

Hence, an aspiring author usually left his hometown, went off to college, lived in a city, and wrote books that mocked small-town people as ugly, petty, and backward. In other words, the practitioner of a craft turned his skills against the community that had raised him. I could have taken that path and for a while seemed to be on it, but somehow I made it back home and stayed and became a small-town author.

Two themes run through this book, and both relate to my struggle to establish myself as an author. They converged like long dusty trails when I returned to the town where I grew up. The first involves voice and place: Who tells the story and where does he come from? The second deals with my attempts to fit writing into a broader context. What is a story? What is art? What should they accomplish, and why does it matter?

When I began my journey, I didn't realize how important those questions would be, nor did I anticipate the answers. They relate to something C. S. Lewis said, that art should attempt to reconstruct patterns and harmonies that were here long before we arrived. We don't create the designs embedded in our world but discover them and try to describe them in the language of our time. The first sentence in the Book of Genesis assures us that a design is there.

I began working on this memoir in 2009, and it has gone through twenty-seven revisions. I continued working on it to give myself something to do during my dedicated morning writing time and to satisfy my curiosity about a particular period of my life.

I understand that some readers will be content to enjoy my Hank books without knowing anything about the guy who wrote them—what he learned or didn't learn in college, which authors he studied, how he developed his writing technique, how difficult a task it was, and how he dealt with failure and rejection.

But some readers will be curious about it. For better or worse, I am part of the Texas Literary Tradition, having been inducted into the Texas Institute of Letters and the Fort Worth Public Library's Texas Literary Hall of Fame. And I've sold quite a few books. It's an unusual story, how that came about.

I would like to express my appreciation to Travis Snyder, editor in chief at Texas Tech University Press, who thought the story was worth sharing with a wider audience, and to editor Christie Perlmutter, who labored to make it better. I'm also grateful to the friends who read the work in manuscript and gave me suggestions on how to improve it: Michael Harter, Sandra Morrow, Kris Erickson, Nancy Pearcey, Dr. Michael Klein, Nathan Johnson, Marian Freeland, Kathryn Presley, John Leicht, Chuck Milner, Britt Hancock, and Peter Forbes.

I am especially indebted to my "students," Nathan Dahlstrom, Nikki Earley, and Mark Erickson, with whom I have carried on a years-long exchange of ideas about writing, dogs, horses, God, children, popular culture, and literature. For me, it has been a very rewarding collaboration.

As always, the biggest bouquet goes to the lady who has shared my life all these years, my wife Kristine. "Her price is far above rubies. . . . She is like the merchants' ships; she bringeth food from afar" (Proverbs 31:10–14).

M-Cross Ranch
Roberts County, Texas
June 2024

SMALL TOWN AUTHOR

PART 1

THE UNIVERSITY YEARS

CHAPTER 1

DENVER AND UT

I was raised in a small farming and ranching community in the Texas Panhandle: Perryton, the county seat of Ochiltree County, 550 miles northwest of the Texas State Capitol and several thousand miles away from the centers of national news and entertainment. It was a quiet, stable environment where families went to church, boys wore short hair, and dogs and cats ran free. It was a nice place to grow up.

As kids, my friends and I spent most of our time playing outside, unsupervised by adults. We played Army, Cowboys, Pirates, Davy Crockett, Tom Sawyer, and Knights of the Round Table, as well as football, baseball, and basketball. We all dreamed of the day we'd become Perryton Rangers.

In our small high school, kids didn't have to specialize in one or two areas. I participated in band, choir, debate, theater, football, track, and student government. In the summer, I worked as a farm and ranch hand and took pride in doing hard work. I didn't want to be soft or lazy.

I gave no thought to college. It wasn't something that people in my family had done or even talked about. Out of four grandparents, seven uncles and aunts, and my parents, only one had graduated from college.

But by the time I reached my senior year in high school, something had changed. It was in the air: Kids like me were expected to go to college. To do otherwise would . . . I don't know, embarrass the family and the hometown, and maybe cause the nation to fall behind the Soviet Union.

The other part of the deal was that, unless your family owned farm and ranch land, you probably wouldn't end up living in Perryton. It had been a nice place to grow up but didn't offer much in the way of excitement or opportunity. The Real World, the one that interested me, was Out There. My mother's family owned ranch land but it lay 350 miles to the south in Gaines County and it wasn't mine.

When I walked across the stage and received my diploma from Superintendent Gilbert Mize in May 1962, I knew I would be going to college and had been accepted at the University of Denver. I didn't have a compelling reason for going north to college, except that Denver wasn't in Texas and I wanted to spend some time out of state. At DU, I found a cosmopolitan mix of students, very few of them from Texas.

DU attracted a number of students from the Northeastern states, and the administration often referred to the school as "the Harvard of the West" (leaving wags to wonder if Harvard bragged about being "the DU of the East"), but its main attraction was that it sat at the feet of the Rocky Mountains, an hour's drive from some of the best skiing in North America.

Many students from the East Coast who failed to get into an Ivy League school went west to DU, where they nursed their sorrows on the slopes or in noisy beer halls in Boulder. I shared a dorm suite with boys from New Hampshire, Pennsylvania, Ohio, Long Island, and Upstate New York. They seemed far more sophisticated than I and made frequent references to a book called *The Catcher in the Rye*. It seemed to be the Bible for Yankee kids who didn't read the Bible.

I was ashamed that I'd never heard of it, so on weekends, while the other lads went off to movies or social events, I stayed in my room and read *The Catcher in the Rye*, as well as *Animal Farm*, *1984*, *Brave New World*, *On the Beach*, and novels by James Baldwin and Richard Wright—books that everyone but me had already read. This allowed me to join conversations about *Catcher in the Rye*, but I chose not to reveal a terrible secret. From start to finish, I had found it boring and depressing. Holden Caulfield didn't capture my heart. He didn't even capture my big toe. If Holden Caulfield had been my college roommate, I would have dragged my mattress down to the basement to avoid him.

Honesty compels me to acknowledge an essay written by Lee Siegel in a journal I respect, *First Things* (June–July 2023), in which he called *Catcher in the Rye* "the most Christian novel ever published" and pointed out that it has sold sixty-five million copies. If I read the book today, I might have a better opinion about it. One hates to be a single voice against sixty-five million.

Across the hall lived two fellows from Cleveland, and I became good friends with both of them. Michael Klein was a serious student and went on to become a pediatric surgeon in Detroit. He introduced me to his friend Mickey, who turned out to be the antithesis of everything in my small-town Baptist experience: an urbanized Yankee, a bohemian artist, a socialist, an atheist, and a hippie before hippies were invented. Against high odds, we became good friends.

I never would have thought that I might find anything in common with a professing nonbeliever. To me, "atheist" was one of the ugliest words in the English language. My faith had taken a turn away from church and toward social issues (Mike Klein and I did volunteer work at a mental hospital in Pueblo, and I worked with a poor family on weekends), but it never would have entered my mind to declare myself an atheist.

I couldn't imagine ever telling my mother that I had become one of those things.

For me, religious faith remained an active, vital topic of discussion, but Mickey had already made up his mind. He had adopted the materialistic-scientific worldview of his father, a physicist, who agreed with Bertrand Russell: "What science cannot discover, mankind cannot know."

Mickey had a zest for life and an outrageous sense of humor, and I couldn't help liking him, but I thought it strange that, while he was rebelling against everything in his middle-class background, he never questioned his father's faith in scientific materialism.

THE UNIVERSITY OF TEXAS

In 1963, after my first year, I transferred to the University of Texas at Austin. DU was a private school and quite expensive, and I thought my educational needs would be served as well by a respected state university whose tuition fee was fifty dollars per semester. Also, my brother Charles was there, finishing up his work for a degree in English, art, or some combination of the two.

When I arrived at UT to register for the fall semester, I had no idea what to declare as a major. Judy Blanton, a friend of my brother, saw at once that I was a lost calf and needed direction. She was a beautiful, vivacious, taffy-blonde sheriff's daughter from a small town in Central Texas and had just completed her degree in a program called Plan II (Plan Two).

Judy was a take-charge kind of girl, and after sizing me up, she declared that I *had* to enroll in Plan II. Like most of the human beings who were alive at that time, I had never heard of Plan II, but people at UT regarded it as something special, an honors program that attempted to provide a small number of young scholars the kind of education they might receive at a liberal arts school such Oberlin, Davidson, Grinnell, or Knox College. The program brought together top students and good professors, placed them in small classes, and gave students the opportunity to pursue their own interests through independent study.

Time proved Judy's instinct to be correct. Plan II was a good program for me, but I wasn't the kind of honors student the Plan II administrators were trying to recruit from the top high schools in Dallas, Houston, Austin, and San Antonio. I had muddled my way through Perryton High School and one year at the University of Denver, and there was nothing in my transcripts or ACT scores to suggest that I would do anything but soil the reputation of an honors program.

That fact didn't bother Judy. She was well connected with the people who ran the program and pulled the right strings to get me accepted on a probationary basis: If my grades fell below a B average, I was out. She made it clear that I had better not let that happen.

Plan II was a demanding course of study. I had always been a slow reader and a lazy student, and my experience at UT wasn't fun or easy. I spent most of my first semester in fear that I was going to flunk Spanish and algebra. It didn't help that UT was an enormous, impersonal campus with a student population of forty thousand—ten times the size of my hometown.

I should have lived in a dorm my first year, but I had gotten the notion that I was above dorm life. I lived off campus in a tiny duplex apartment, next door to a Palestinian Arab named Taha Zagmut, one of hundreds of Arabs who flocked to UT to study petroleum engineering. He tried to tutor me in algebra, and I helped him with English.

He was a pleasant fellow until the subject of "Ees-rah-ell" reared its head. At the mention of Israel, he was transformed. His black eyes glazed over, and he began screaming about Zionist propaganda and Jewish conspiracies. If I dared suggest that America was more than a Jewish colony, he would stare at me and a wolf's smile would form on his lips. It said, "Ah, so they've gotten to you, too." This was the first of many episodes that indicated the spirit of social division and upheaval in the air.

During the fall semester, I had hardly any social life. After class, I went to Batts Hall, checked out tapes in the language lab, and spent hours listening to Spanish conversations. (It worked. I made a B in the course and became fairly fluent in Spanish.) When the lab closed, I trudged back to my dingy little apartment to resume my war with algebra, or to read bleak short stories for my course in American literature.

My social life consisted of attending an occasional movie, going to UT football games (Coach Darrell Royal's Longhorns won the National Championship in 1963), eating a Top Chop steak and a slice of banana cream pie at the Nighthawk Restaurant, and sharing brittle ecumenical moments with Taha and, sometimes, his friends from Iraq and Syria.

PSYCHOLOGY

About halfway through my first semester, I awoke to the fact that I was unhappy, not a normal condition for me and not something I felt I could discuss with my parents. I had heard that the Student Health Center kept psychologists on staff, so I made an appointment with one of them.

At my first session, the doctor tapped his pencil, stared at me for an hour, and said nothing. The most obvious and helpful advice he might have given ("Why don't you join a church?") he didn't offer. Apparently, he expected me to talk, so I talked. The pattern persisted through five sessions, and I began to realize that he was never going to say anything. This was it.

Those sessions revealed that I was a small-town kid, adrift in a huge university, living in fear of failing two courses and needing some human companionship—all of which I had known before submitting to counseling. At that point, a thought flashed in my mind: *The doctor was in worse shape than I was.*

I stopped going to counseling and didn't set foot in the Student Health Center again until two years later when, early one Sunday morning, I had to deliver a friend to the emergency room. Bill and his girlfriend had just broken up and he tried to drown himself in a bottle of gin. He almost succeeded. Like me, Bill had been raised Southern Baptist and had never spent any time thinking about the ingredients in a Tom Collins. All he knew was that it tasted good and helped numb the ache of his broken heart.

Bill and I had become friends in the university a cappella choir. He had a fine tenor voice and was scheduled to sing a solo at the eleven o'clock service at University Methodist Church. When I lugged him into the emergency room, I began to wonder if that was going to work out.

At nine o'clock, his eyes were crooked and his chin rested on the rim of a Health Center commode. At ten, he was stretched out on a gurney, ash-faced and clammy of skin, wondering why nobody back in Louisiana had told him that gin is a toxic substance when taken in large quantities.

The nurse gave him a shot of something (not gin) and sent him home. He missed the service, and I doubt that church officials ever heard the straight story.

But back to psychology. My experience with the Health Center psychologist had turned out badly, but I couldn't bring myself to dismiss the entire profession on the performance of one practitioner. Maybe psychology had more to offer and could give me valuable insights into . . . well, dating, for example.

I hadn't fared well in that department. Surely, in a student population of forty thousand, there must have been a few young ladies who weren't neurotic and unhappy, but I hadn't found them. Neurosis seemed almost epidemic—even fashionable—in the College of Arts and Sciences, so perhaps a young blade's best hope of finding the girl of his dreams was to broaden his understanding of human behavior.

I enrolled in a course that sounded promising: Introduction to Psychology. The professor, Dr. Ira Iscoe, was a delightful man: alert, intelligent, cynical, and funny. I enjoyed his lectures, and if I had been dating pigeons or lab rats, I might have gotten some valuable insights.

To my amazement, this course in psychology had nothing to say about human beings, only rodents and birds and how they responded to food pellets and electrical shocks.

CLASSES AND PROFESSORS

One of the bright spots of my college experience was Paul F. Boller's two-semester course in American intellectual history. Boller, a visiting professor from Southern Methodist University (SMU), had three degrees and a Phi Beta Kappa key from Yale and was "old school" in his approach to education. He thought that students should read and that professors should *teach*, a quaint custom the tenured nobility at UT didn't always embrace.

He ran the course as a graduate seminar and didn't use a textbook. In the fall semester, we had to read fourteen books, a formidable challenge for me, a slow reader.

Dr. Boller was a published author, the first I had ever met, and he considered writing one of the skills that educated people should possess. He assigned essays and rarely used multiple choice examinations, and I did well in his class. He actually *read* our essays, graded them himself, and left plenty of red ink in the margins. He graded hard—no grade inflation, no curve.

Most of his students made a C, a crushing experience for those who had waltzed through Spring Branch and Highland Park High Schools with perfect marks. In Boller's class, a good performance earned a B. To extract an A out of him, you not only had to master the subject but also to express it well in your writing. I made an A both semesters, which shocked me as much as the C's shocked the better students.

My junior year, I took a Shakespeare course under a young instructor named Alan Friedman who had just come to UT after finishing his doctorate at the University of Rochester. Friedman looked about twenty-five, had a solemn narrow face, wore owlish black glasses, and was an outstanding teacher. His quiet manner gave no hint that he would be a ferocious grader. His multiple-choice tests were fiendishly difficult, and out of a class of thirty-five, he gave only one A—not to me.

I enjoyed the course and loved the idea of reading Shakespeare. It seemed so cultured and civilized, but early on, I began to realize that, for me at least, Shakespeare was unreadable. Friedman suggested that I listen to the plays in the language lab and follow along in the text. *King Lear* almost wore me out. As I recall, it ran more than three hours. I had a wild romp through the wonderland of Shakespeare and never worked harder for a Gentleman's B.

I have pleasant memories of a Plan II seminar class I took under classics professor Donald Carne-Ross, a bearded Englishman with impish eyes and a very dry sense of humor. He often smoked a pipe during his lectures and seemed the perfect embodiment of a rumpled British intellectual. The course was called "The Hero in Literature," and Carne-Ross gave us a heavy load of reading: the *Epic of Gilgamesh*, the *Enuma Elish*, the *Prose Edda*, the *Iliad*, the *Odyssey*, the *Aeneid*, *Beowulf*, and James Joyce's *A Portrait of the Artist as a Young Man*.

JOHN SILBER

I also took a year-long introduction to philosophy under the notorious John Silber, one of the top-gun professors in the Plan II program. He was already a legend by the time I got to UT.

He had been an early and loud opponent of segregation and the death penalty and was one of the writing stars at *The Texas Observer*. His reputation grew in years to come, when he moved on to become the president of Boston University and a candidate for governor of Massachusetts. He lost that race but succeeded in starting fires of controversy all over the state.

Silber was a one-armed Kantian scholar with a doctorate from Yale. He was small of stature, youthful in appearance, pugnacious in manner, and had an amazing pair of blue eyes that came at you like lasers. He inspired more extremes of emotion than any professor I ever encountered. The faculty at Boston University considered him a despot, but former US Secretary of Education William Bennett, who earned a doctorate under Silber, called him one of the best teachers he ever had.

He was a man who seemed to fear nothing, least of all what anyone thought of him. "The truly courageous do not live in anxiety from morning to night. They are calm because they know who they are, what their profession is, and its duties. In that knowledge, they do their duty with equanimity" (Silber, 1989, 258). One surmised that Silber had a strong sense of who he was and it included an appetite for storms, because they followed him from room to room, building to building, and state to state.

Somehow, he stayed married to the same woman, Kathryn, and they had eight children together. As a young novelist-to-be, I often passed time trying to construct stories about people I encountered, but even my active imagination couldn't build a story that involved John Silber mowing the grass or wiping a smudge of peanut butter off the face of a child.

His debating tactics combined the Socratic method with the savagery of a Mongolian warrior. If he thought he was right (and there never seemed much doubt about that), he considered it his duty to take the flesh off the bones of an opponent, then grind up the bones for fertilizer.

I remember one class session in particular, a lecture with a hundred fifty honors students (a small lecture class at UT). We had been told to read a book by Bishop Berkeley. As usual, Silber called on a student and began asking questions about the text, a technique he had learned during the one year he had spent at Yale Law School. In my class, every student lived in fear of being called upon.

On this occasion, he chose a philosophy major named Larry who regarded himself as brilliant and carried his learning with an air of smirking self-assurance. Unfortunately for Larry, he had come to class unprepared. Silber's eyes flashed with unholy light, and he began an interrogation that would have been admired in the cellars of the KGB's Lubyanka prison. It took him about five minutes to remove the skin and flesh from Larry's quaking bones, but he didn't stop. The massacre went on for *the entire hour*.

The rest of us stared at the floor, thanking God (or whoever was running the universe) that we hadn't been called on, and praying that when Silber finished with poor Larry, he wouldn't start looking around for fresh meat. It got so bad, several girls started crying and some students got up and left. The rest of us were afraid to move. When the hour finally ended, we hurried to the exits, hushed and pale.

For the rest of the semester, Larry left his smirk at the door and made it a point to prepare for class, so Silber's flogging probably made him a better student. The incident certainly added to the Silber Legend, but I don't think it was his finest hour. I suspect that twenty-five years after they graduated, his students remembered more about John Silber than they did about Plato, Bergson, Kant, Kierkegaard, and Bishop Berkeley. That's not the way it's supposed to work.

After college, I exchanged several letters with him and naturally they were feisty, both his and mine. Opening one of Silber's letters was like turning the crank on a jack-in-the box: out popped a spring-loaded boxing glove that bashed you in the nose. I'll never forget the opening line in one of his letters: "John: I see you're still a young horse's ass." He was right, of course.

Silber died in 2012 at the age of 86. He was one of a kind.

CHOIR

It was my good fortune to grow up in a home, church, and school that placed a high value on music. In high school, I sang in a choir directed by Cloys Webb, a gifted musician who somehow coaxed beautiful sounds out of teenagers who were listening to Little Richard and Elvis Presley on their car radios. He produced outstanding choirs, and by the time I graduated from high school, I had learned choral discipline and was a pretty good singer.

In the fall of 1964, I decided to audition for the UT a cappella choir. Most of the people in that choir were music majors, and I didn't have much confidence that I would qualify, but three kids from Perryton had succeeded (Frances Crawford, Tom Ellzey, and John Ellzey) and they encouraged me to give it a shot.

When I went to the audition, the assistant director said they needed second tenors, not basses or baritones, so I auditioned as a second tenor and got accepted. The choir, directed by Dr. Morris Beachy, rehearsed two afternoons a week, two hours per session. In the spring of 1965, we gave several performances in Mexico City at the Academy of San Carlos.

It was an excellent choir, good enough to have sung Morten Lauridsen's *O magnum mysterium*, only Lauridsen hadn't written it yet. I was proud to be part of that choir and to have sung under Dr. Beachy.

WRITING

In my senior year, my interest in writing began to bloom. During the fall semester, I took advantage of the Plan II program's independent study option and wrote a long one-act play under the supervision of Alan Friedman, the same professor who had given me a B in my course on Shakespeare. My play was a dreary tale of existential angst, humorless and depressing, exactly the sort of rubbish a budding intellectual was supposed to be writing in 1965, and Friedman thought it deserved an A.

He delivered this news with an air of sadness, because he regarded the giving of an A as almost as unpleasant as getting a tooth pulled. To ease him through the ordeal, I took him and his wife out to supper at a nice restaurant overlooking Lake Austin. By the end of the evening, he was able to smile again.

The next semester, I did another independent study course under William H. Goetzmann, a Pulitzer Prize–winning historian. This time I wrote a three-act play, based on the life of Eugene V. Debs, and met with Dr. Goetzmann only three times. He must have thought it was an ambitious task for an undergraduate and gave me an A, but I'm sure that anyone with a background in theater would have judged it a bad play.

I also got a job writing a weekly editorial column for *The Daily Texan*. Under the editorship of Kay Northcott (years later, she became editor of the *Texas Observer*), the *Texan* was regarded as an example of high-quality student journalism. It was also a trumpet of undergraduate hubris. I made good use of this forum, writing columns that tended to be shrill, incendiary, and disrespectful to all figures of authority, from the board of regents to God himself.

I enjoyed lobbing cans of hairspray into quiet fires, but never paused to think that, in maturity, I might hope and pray that nobody ever poked through those ashes. A writer's greatest fear should be that the words of his youth might actually become immortal. If I read those pieces today, I would be embarrassed.

POLITICS

In the spring semester of my junior year, I was seized by the notion that the school would be a better place if I got myself elected to the student senate. I must have forgotten a nugget of wisdom I had learned at the University of Denver, where I had dabbled in student politics: If you get elected to an office, *you have to attend all the meetings.*

It is hard to look back on college politics without drifting into satire. To a jaded adult, all student campaigns appear silly. It's a bit like listening to a high school band playing their school song—the honking saxophones, squeaking clarinets, and thumping drums—and wondering how anyone could regard it as anything but a parody of school patriotism. But at certain times and ages, we all take it seriously.

Social ferment was in the air at UT, and I had sprouted a defiant little beard and allowed my hair to grow fairly long. In Austin's humid climate, it leavened into an unruly puff of curls that had lain dormant during my high school years in the arid Panhandle. Austin introduced me to my curly hair.

I don't recall the specific issues of my campaign, but I'm guessing that they all funneled down to one: Student government had been taken over by shallow frat rats and sorority girls. A great university needed the voice of an independent lion who had read Plato's *Republic*, who could represent all the disenfranchised students in the departments of philosophy, classics, and literature, and who would transform the student senate into a solemn deliberative body.

Early in the campaign, someone suggested that I seek the advice of a fellow who actually knew something about student politics: Jay Westbrook. I called him and arranged a meeting. Jay wore a suit and tie (very unusual in those times) and had the confident air of a political operative who had guided many student campaigns from a back room.

I don't remember the advice he gave me (it didn't help, I lost the election), but I do remember meeting his friend, a tall young man with penetrating blue eyes: Whitley Strieber. Years later, he became a successful author, and I read *Communion*, a book about his abduction by "visitors." It was a strange and disturbing book.

I ran an earnest campaign and tried to whip up enthusiasm among students in the College of Arts and Sciences, many of whom regarded the whole thing as a massive irrelevance. I didn't have a lot of money to spend on printing, so I depended on volunteer help. We created our own posters at poster parties.

It was at one of those events that I met the love of my life, the woman who would become my wife, Kristine Dykema. She came with a friend of mine, a big, happy engineering student from California. (Engineers didn't have to read Sartre or Samuel Beckett or Jean Genet, so many of them were happy.)

I noticed that Kris was tall, dark, shapely, and beautiful. I remember thinking that my friend was dating above his level and probably didn't deserve her. Beyond that, I didn't pay much attention to Kris, an act of carelessness I can't explain, except that I was preoccupied with my political destiny. My time would have been better spent flirting with her and trying to steal her away from Teddy Bear, the big happy engineer.

My opponent in the student senate race was an attractive Pi Phi from Houston who had a clear understanding of student politics: If she was the candidate of the Greeks, she would win. It was that simple.

The Greeks had refined campus politics down to a few basic steps: Spend a lot of money on printed signs and posters, use underclassmen pledges to plaster them all over campus and in store windows on the Drag, and turn out the vote. My opponent ran no campaign. She didn't hold a "position on the issues" or make speeches or try to convince anyone that she was intelligent. (I did.) On election day, she sat in a booth on the mall with her sorority sisters and gave out cookies. I lost the race for student senate and the university plunged into another year of darkness under a Greek regime.

There is a footnote to this campaign. Somewhere in the yellowing files of *The Daily Texan* resides a page with photographs of all the candidates in the race for student senate. My portrait shows a somber young man, serious but not crazy, whose chin and cheeks are fluffed with a downy boy's beard.

On the same page is a photograph of a clean-shaven, short-haired fraternity boy named Richard Friedman, whom Texans knew later as Kinky: founder of a rock band called The Texas Jewboys, author of detective novels, columnist, humorist, and occasional candidate for governor of Texas.

Kinky and I never crossed paths at UT. I met him thirty years later at book-and-author functions. By that time, he was writing detective novels and had evolved into his identity as a postmodern cowboy, wearing boots, black hat, and black frock coat, and smoking a big black cigar in places where smoking wasn't permitted.

On several occasions, I tried to strike up a conversation with him but had no success. It was very odd. I got the feeling that he had become an actor wearing a costume and performing in a play called "Everything's a Joke." He was a joke, I was a joke, the book conference was a joke . . . politics, religion, music, cowboys, librarians, manners, literature, love . . . everything. He'd invented the play and he controlled it. If you wanted to talk to Kinky, you had to audition for a role and stick with his theatrical design. If you didn't, if you tried to exit the format . . . well, that was proof you didn't get the joke.

Those encounters left me puzzled. If there was a Richard Friedman behind the Kinky mask, I didn't get to meet him.

STUDENT RADICALS

Even those of us who were alive and alert during the sixties have a hard time comprehending the magnitude of change that occurred in the span of a few short years. It was enormous.

When I left home in 1962 and went off to college, I had never heard of race riots or antiwar protests and had never known anyone who used illegal drugs. In dating situations, the boy always knew the answer to the perennial question: no.

Divorce and out-of-wedlock babies were almost unheard of and were considered scandalous.

When parents sent their children off to college, they assumed that the school would provide parental oversight and that it would affirm the Judeo-Christian values that, since the founding of the nation, most Americans had accepted as normal. By the middle of the 1960s, those circumstances had changed.

What happened to us? Os Guinness was a British scholar who studied under Francis Schaeffer at the L'Abri community in Switzerland and earned a doctorate at Oxford University. He pointed to the assassination of President John Kennedy in 1963 as the event that started the ferment. During the sixties, Guinness traveled around the US and made these observations:

> [The rebellion] protested effectively against mindless materialism and intellectual equivocation. Moderation had slipped into mediocrity. . . . Blind spots, such as racial bigotry, urban poverty, militarism, and environmental disregard, were exposed and then attacked, ostensibly in the name of a stronger morality and a higher idealism. . . . All the traditional sources of legitimacy received a mauling and were left for dead. . . . But as one observer wrote astutely, the counterculture was "a revolt of the unoppressed" (Guinness, 1994, 378–79).

It was a rich kids' radicalism.

I seldom went to church while I was at UT and rebelled against some of the values of my parents but didn't drift as far from my roots as some of my contemporaries, who seemed to have severed all ties with their parents and home communities and were sailing into waters beyond the horizon.

I was never *that* angry about whatever we were so angry about, and I learned not to trust Marxist radicals. Whatever the flaws of the Southern Baptists, I would have preferred being stranded in a lifeboat with a bunch of evangelicals to anyone who belonged to the Students for a Democratic Society, which had a strong presence at UT. As a group, they struck me as dishonest, arrogant, manipulative, bitter, self-absorbed, slightly crazy, and bent on some sort of destruction.

Some of them thought of themselves as writers and poets, or maybe the proper term would be Lonely Mad Artists. I don't know where the paradigm came from (jazz culture, the Civil Rights movement, leftist politics, the Beat Generation poets, Ingmar Bergman movies, or all of them rolled together), but Hemingway was one of their icons.

They cultivated the appearance of anger and devil-may-care rebellion, and drinking was an important part of the process, as it had been for Hemingway. They had their own tables at the student union where they puffed unfiltered cigarettes, flicked the hair out of their eyes, and glared at the engineers and business majors who didn't know that they were all going to DIE. They took turns reading angry poems that had no rhyme or meter, because rhyme and meter were only sops for bourgeois sheep who didn't realize that they were ALL going to DIE.

It was a bizarre model, the Lonely Mad Artist. I can't imagine applying it to any other craft or trade. Does anyone want his house wired by an angry, alcoholic electrician, or to fly in a commercial jet whose pilot reminds the passengers that they're all going to DIE? Someday the culture of the Lonely Mad Artist might become fertile ground for satire and humor. Or maybe it will always remain just sad.

I never became part of their group. Even though I was creeping toward the idea of becoming an author, I retained a small-town kid's wariness about burning bridges and diving off into dark places. I didn't hate my parents or my country, and I already knew that we're all going to die. I had learned it in a Southern Baptist church, though I never would have admitted that anywhere in Travis County.

I had a feeling the Artists were better at drinking than writing. Writing is not something you do at a noisy table in the student union or at Scholz Beer Garden. In later years, I looked for their names in bookstores and on lists of Texas authors but never saw one of them mentioned.

Maybe they became unhappy alcoholic English professors who roared and foamed about the stupidity of the tax-paying middle class, or maybe they just died young, proving that they were right all along.

CHAPTER 2

THE DANCE

In September 1965, after spending a summer in New York, I lived in an off-campus apartment and took my evening meals at College House, which served as a gathering place for people who were too liberal in their politics to feel at home in a fraternity or sorority but not radical enough to seek companionship in the shadowy fringe that was brooding over Marx and Frantz Fanon.

Some thought of themselves as artists, some as intellectuals. They were readers and thinkers, good students, and I suspect that many of them went on to pursue graduate degrees and became college professors.

At six o'clock every evening, fifty or sixty College House residents and associate members (who, like me, didn't live there) gathered in the dining room and ate at long tables. After the meal, we listened to a guest speaker, then spent an hour or more discussing the topic.

One evening, we heard a presentation by a young man who belonged to the Society of Friends (Quakers) and who argued the case for pacifism. Even at this early date, many residents of College House opposed the war in Vietnam, and the speaker's pacifist views received a supportive response.

I waited for someone to raise the obvious questions about pacifism, but it appeared that the speaker was going to make it through the program without a challenge. So I asked, "Are you saying that if someone broke into your home and threatened your wife and children, you wouldn't defend them?"

"That is my position, yes."

"Pardon me, but that sounds crazy."

I didn't mean to be rude, but there was still enough of the country boy in me to rebel at the logical consequences of dogmatic pacifism. It struck me as indefensible and immoral. If you allow bad guys to bump off good guys, you'll end up with a rotten society every time.

I caught a few icy glares from the students around me, but one member of the audience was applauding in silence: Kristine Dykema. She lived at College House, and my question impressed her. Years later, she told me that right then, she knew that she would end up marrying me.

Had she told me, I would have been stunned. I had hardly noticed her, but one evening, weeks later, I did. She was an unusually beautiful and graceful woman. Her dark features and last name, Dykema, made me think she might be Greek, Lebanese, or Jewish.

I made my way over to her and slipped into the serving line behind her. We talked for a while and I finally got around to asking, "Do you have a telephone?" She smiled and said, "Yes." I waited. She didn't give me the number and it made me so mad, I stormed away. *I wasn't going to beg for her phone number!*

The next day I was eating lunch in the student union with a friend, Olin Clemmons. I told him about this girl who, for a moment, had caught my eye: "But she had her chance and she blew it."

At that moment, someone slipped up behind me and placed her hands over my eyes. When she removed them, I looked around and saw HER . . . and melted. She stayed just long enough to give me her phone number. When she left, Olin flashed a smirk. "What were you saying?" We shared a laugh. I had been turned wrong side out and Olin knew it.

Later, I asked Kris why she hadn't given me her phone number the first time. She said, "Well, you didn't ask for it. You asked if I *had* one. I didn't want to assume too much, and you should have been more specific."

I began calling her in the evenings and we had long, pleasant conversations. I learned that her mother had been born in Scotland and her father's people were "black Dutch," a mix of Dutch and Spanish blood. She'd been raised Presbyterian, enjoyed singing, and was taking a class in modern dance. Her family had lived in Michigan until she was twelve, then moved to Dallas. She had graduated from Thomas Jefferson High School and was studying interior design at UT.

When I asked her out for a date, I learned that I wasn't the only blade on campus who had noticed her charm and beauty. She had a long list of suitors, and I had to wait my turn, which had a souring effect on my disposition. To me, it seemed obvious that she needed to get rid of those louts and spend hours and hours every day staring into my eyes and laughing at my witticisms.

To that she said, "You're too pushy."

Indeed I was. Kris was like no girl I had encountered at UT. She had poise, grace, intelligence, and depth but wasn't desperate to reveal everything she knew. There was a deep honesty about her and wisdom that came from quiet places. She was comfortable with herself, and I felt comfortable being with her.

We had a few dates, but not enough to suit me. She kept reminding me that she was taking five courses and needed to study at night, and that she'd been dating those other boys long before she'd met me.

Something had to be done about this.

At Christmas break, I made the long drive from Austin to the Panhandle, exactly 550 miles from the UT campus to my parents' house in Perryton, and that gave me eleven hours to think and scheme. Somewhere around Guthrie, where a traveler might begin to notice the bite of Panhandle winter, I came up with an idea.

Kris had told me that she loved to dance and was enrolled in a modern dance class in the drama department. *I would write a dance drama, with Kris dancing the lead role!*

ADAM, ADAM

Most people who write dance dramas are theater majors. At the very least, they know something about choreography. I knew nothing about it. I'd grown up in a church that didn't approve of dancing and came from Protestant stock that didn't have the time or the genetic material for it.

No problem. I knew that Kris could handle it.

I rolled into Perryton around eleven o'clock that night. My father had gone to bed at ten, a ritual he observed regardless of who was there or who was coming to visit, be it me or the Queen of England. At 10 p.m., he rose from his chair, invited his guests to stay as long as they wished and to turn out the lights when they left, and went off to bed.

In college, I had become a night owl and at ten o'clock, I

was ready to plunge into long, deep discussions about . . . well, Life and Art and Religion. When I tried to explain this to my father, he would say, "Good. I'll see you in the morning." He had a business to open on Main Street.

My mother was just as predictable the other way. No matter how late I arrived, she stayed up to welcome me home. When I drove in from Austin that night, we visited for an hour or so, and when she retired, I went into the study where my father kept his Yamaha grand piano. I sat down at the table where he played solitaire, worked his crossword puzzles, composed letters, and studied the Bible, and began writing on a legal pad, blocking out scenes and writing dialogue.

By the time I went to bed at four o'clock, I had sketched out the rough draft of a dance drama called *Adam, Adam*.

No copy of that script has survived, but it remains a memory. It had three characters: a male named Adam, a female who personified Life and fertility, and a female who personified Death. The two female characters had only a few spoken lines and most of the action centered on the choreography, as they danced around Adam. The Life character danced with a lighted candle. At the end of the play, she passed the flame to the Death character, who blew it out.

The mood of the play was biblical and rather dark. Maybe it drew from Sunday school memories of Job, Lamentations, and Ecclesiastes. As novelist Herman Wouk observed, parts of the Old Testament express despair with black eloquence not bettered in modern literature.

I spent several days revising the play, typed it up, and mailed a copy to Kris in Dallas. I called her and said, "We're going to put on that play and produce it ourselves. I don't know where we'll do the show, but we'll find a place. You'll dance the lead and we'll get Ellen Deacon to take the other part. I'll do Adam's part."

I had given the Adam character some lines of dialogue but *no dancing*.

After the Christmas break, we threw ourselves into the project. Kris and Ellen made their costumes and worked on their makeup and choreography. They might have gotten some outside help but did most of it on their own.

Meanwhile, I created a musical score, drawing from my collection of classical LPs and those of my roommate, Lawrie Ellzey. I have forgotten the music I chose for Kris's part (it was warm and melodic), but I remember my selection for the character of Death: Ralph Vaughan Williams's frigid and forbidding *Sinfonia Antarctica*.

Lawrie and I grew up together in Perryton and shared a small house east of campus. The location is now buried beneath a temple erected to honor a local politician who spent billions of other people's money on buildings, highways, and parks, and put his name on them: Lyndon B. Johnson.

Lawrie was working on a doctorate in quantum chemistry at UT and played an important role in our production. He was one of those fellows who couldn't dance, sing, or act but knew where to get a top-of-the-line Ampex tape recorder and how to wire one electronic device into another, hook it all up to a sound system, and make everything work—exactly the technical skills we needed.

After we had rehearsed the play for several weeks, I got permission to use the stage at the Wesleyan Student Center on Guadalupe Street, a short distance from the UT student union. We made our own posters and tacked them on bulletin boards around campus. We put on two performances, one on Friday night and one on Saturday. Lawrie was backstage, running the lights and sound.

Today, looking back, I find it amazing that we ever thought

we could do such a thing. We drew a decent crowd both nights and the girls gave flawless performances. Kris was spectacular, grace personified. Watching her, I fell even deeper in love.

As if by design, our rehearsal schedule forced a new reality upon Kris's old boyfriends: they were *out*, I was in. Heh heh.

My father drove all the way from Perryton to attend the Saturday performance. I don't recall his saying much about my script or acting skills, but he sure took notice of Kris: "That's quite a girl." About six months later, when she spent a few days with us in Perryton, he crooked his finger at me and led me back into his bedroom.

He closed the door and said, "If you don't marry that girl, you're crazy."

At the time, I considered myself light-years away from the responsibilities of marriage and family, and the very thought of it caused me to break out in a sweat. But I didn't forget his advice, which slashed like sharp steel through fog and ambiguity and went right to the heart of things.

It was an important message for a father to communicate to his son, the most valuable piece of advice he ever gave me. And he did it with only eight words. Professional writers spend years trying to learn such thrift with language.

CHAPTER 3

THE TOWER

In the summer of 1966 I was taking several courses so that I could finish up my degree at the University of Texas. On August 1, a typical hot, breathless, sweltering day in Austin, I ate lunch in the student union cafeteria with Kristine Dykema, the Dallas girl who would become my wife a year later.

I had a government class at one o'clock, and Kris walked with me to Garrison Hall. We crossed the wide mall, right below the three-hundred-foot Tower building that was the dominant structure on campus (the grumpy J. Frank Dobie complained that it resembled a giant phallus) and talked for a while outside the west entrance of Garrison Hall.

At one o'clock, I went to my class on the second floor and Kris walked back across the mall to the student union. As she approached the door, a man flung it open and pulled her inside. "Someone is on the Tower, shooting people!"

Unknown to us, a man named Charles Whitman had entered the Tower building, taken an elevator to the observation deck on the top floor, murdered a university employee and a tourist, and began firing a high-powered scoped rifle at pedestrians on the mall.

From the west window in my classroom, we had a clear view of the mall and the Tower. The teaching assistant was standing in front of the window, lecturing about Thomas Hobbes. We heard popping sounds outside. At first the teacher ignored them, then smirked and said, "The fraternity boys must be doing something on campus today." We assumed we were hearing firecrackers.

An ashen-faced man entered the room and motioned for the instructor to come. They spoke in whispers and our teacher, stunned, told us to get out of our chairs and sit on the floor against the north wall. Someone with a gun was on the Tower and had shot a man in the Business-Economics Building, right next door to Garrison Hall. Through our window, if we had chosen to look, we could have seen bodies lying on the mall.

Moments later, as we sat on the floor, we heard the loud gunfire—inside our building! At this point, we had no idea what was going on, who was shooting or why, or how many people were involved. As far as we knew, "they" had entered Garrison Hall and were shooting into classrooms. Much to our relief, a man came to our door and reported that the gunfire was coming from highway patrol officers who were firing at the Tower from a third-floor window.

The siege ended about an hour and a half later when, we were told, police had killed the sniper. Nobody knew the final death count until later (fourteen, plus Whitman and two of his family members), but we knew it had been a massacre. I left Garrison Hall and walked across the mall to the Student Union Building to look for Kris. University employees were hosing blood stains off the mall.

The university community was stunned for days, as we read newspaper accounts, watched the endless news coverage on television, and tried to answer the obvious questions: Who was Charles Whitman and why had he brought this monstrous evil to our campus?

The thing that made the Whitman story particularly creepy was that it yielded no simple answers, only a trail of clues that really didn't explain anything. Whitman's father had a violent temper and a history of abuse; his wife had left him just a few months before the shootings. Charles had not lived up to his own expectations, had been troubled by depression, had gone to counseling, and had taken Valium. He was struggling under a heavy course load at UT. He took Dexedrine and sometimes went days without sleeping. He hated his father.

After his death, an autopsy revealed the presence of a small tumor in his brain. He seemed to have no firm foundation of morals. Some commentators suggested that he was a psychopath, a man without a conscience.

To this day, more than fifty years later, nobody knows for certain why a crew-cut ex-Marine, former Eagle Scout engineering student did what he did:

> On the night of July 31, went to his mother's apartment, strangled her with a piece of hose, and left a note beside her body saying, "I just took my mother's life. I am very upset for having done it."
>
> Returned to the apartment he shared with Kathy, his wife of four years, stabbed her five times in the chest, killing her, and then wrote notes to his father and brothers.
>
> On the morning of August 1, filled a footlocker with

rifles, pistols, ammunition, food, and supplies; rented a two-wheeled dolly to carry the chest; rode the elevator to the twenty-seventh floor of the Tower building; and lugged the chest up three flights of stairs to the observation platform.

Bludgeoned to death the receptionist and began firing a scoped 6mm rifle, pot-shooting random targets below on the mall and Guadalupe Street, his first victim being a pregnant woman.

Continued his reign of terror for ninety-six minutes, until Austin police stormed the observation deck and killed him with a shotgun blast.

In the days and nights after the massacre, those of us left behind tried to absorb the magnitude of what had occurred. I wanted to go home (many students did go home), but where was home? I had become a man of the world, only to find that the world had acquired a level of horror and disorder that I had never suspected.

So much changed in such a short period of time. In a matter of hours, the unheard-of had walked into our lives. The unthinkable had moved in next door. The day after Charles Whitman's rampage on the Tower, America was not the same place it had been before.

And so it remains. School shootings and mass murders have become almost commonplace in the Land of the Free and the Home of the Brave . . . and we, who fancy ourselves as the smartest people who ever lived, are still trying to understand why.

Some observers have suggested that if we don't approve of mass murder, maybe we should say so: "*Thou shalt not kill.*"

CHAPTER 4

HARVARD

"I'm going to leave old Texas now. / I have no use for the Longhorn cow."

—Traditional song

In my senior year at UT, I was involved in several community-related projects that were sponsored by the university YMCA, a benevolent organization that had retained a faint smell of the Christian fire. Frank Wright, the director of the Y, was a Quaker, or as he put it, a "Friend," the designation for a member of the Society of Friends.

I attended a few of their worship services, where thirty adults sat in silence for an hour. They seldom had music and when they did, it came from earnest students who plucked nylon-string guitars and sang protest songs.

This was quite a contrast to the high-decibel Southern Baptist services of my youth, and at first it appealed to me—gentle people ruminating on social justice. After a while, though, it seemed only dreary and slightly ridiculous. It struck me as no accident that the Quaker church, once a strong force in Anglo American affairs, had withered down to a twig.

One day at the Y, someone pointed to a brochure that had been posted on the bulletin board. It said that the Theological Education Fund, a Rockefeller Brothers foundation program, was taking applications for a fellowship that would allow the recipients to spend a year studying at a seminary of their choice. The only requirement, beyond the usual academic standards, was that the student had to consider going into a church-related career.

I had stopped going to church and had been pretty thoroughly hosed down by secular ideas at UT, so it seemed unlikely that I would end up doing church work, but I was willing to consider it and to devote a year to the study of theology, a subject that had been missing from my "broad liberal arts education" at UT.

I filled out the application and won a fellowship. At the Y, I had met a student named Kurt Pocsi, who was on leave of absence from Harvard Divinity School. He insisted that I apply to HDS and offered to write a letter of recommendation.

I couldn't imagine that a branch of the lofty Harvard University would have any use for me. My grades weren't all that good, just a bit better than a B average, and my SAT and GRE scores echoed the verdict that I wasn't an exceptional student. But I filled out the application, sent it to Harvard, and was accepted, probably because I wrote good essays. I'm sure it didn't hurt that I already had a fellowship and wasn't begging for money.

This was an exciting moment for a young man who had grown up in a little Texas town where, during the Kennedy administration, we heard a great deal about Harvard. One of my reasons for going there was to find out if a small-town kid from Texas could compete in such a place.

SEMINOLE

In August, I finished my degree at UT (I didn't attend the commencement ceremony) and decided to spend a few days with my widowed grandmother, Mabel Sherman Curry, in Seminole, Texas. She was the matriarch of Mother's Sherman-Curry clan of ranch people in West Texas and a living link to a frontier past Mother had told me about when I was young.

In a few weeks, I would be leaving Texas and starting a new adventure in Cambridge, Massachusetts. I had a suspicion that I would end up staying on the East Coast and must have felt a need to touch base with my roots. Grandmother was excited and urged me to visit.

I made the long drive from Austin to Seminole, arriving in time for a big supper of fried steak. After Grandmother went to bed, I drifted into my grandfather's library and spent several hours browsing through his large collection of books about Texas and the Southwest. I pulled out a volume with a faded brown spine: *Charles Goodnight: Cowman and Plainsman* by J. Evetts Haley.

I had heard of the book but had never read it. On the first page I saw a note in my grandfather's handwriting: "B. B. Curry's book. Bought from J. Evetts Haley 1937." A glance at the copyright page confirmed that this was a first edition, published by the Boston firm of Houghton Mifflin in 1936.

I sat down in a comfortable chair and began reading. On page 49 I was surprised to see a checkmark in the margin—surprised because, although Grampy Buck had often marked his place in a book with a strip of toilet paper or a check from the Seminole State Bank, he had seldom written in the margins.

His pencil mark drew my attention to a passage that began: "On their way out to open country, [the Comanches] came to where a man by the name of Sherman had settled on Stagg Prairie, in the western edge of Parker County."

I had stumbled upon the half-forgotten story about the death of my great-great-grandmother, Martha Sherman, in November 1860.

When I was young, Mother told me about a distant relative, Mrs. Sherman, who had been "killed by Indians." Mother was a good storyteller but not much of a historian. Her tales seldom came with dates or specific locations, so in my young mind, they had the quality of myth. I was never sure when, where, or if this incident had actually occurred, until that night in 1966.

In November 1860, Ezra and Martha Sherman were living on the edge of the settled frontier, in eastern Palo Pinto County, west of Weatherford—a very dangerous place to be because the formidable Comanches were on a bloody rampage.

The Shermans had three children and were trying to scratch out a living from the soil. One of the children, Joe, was Grandmother Curry's father, my great-grandfather. He was hiding in the brushes and watched as the Comanches captured Martha, who was nine months pregnant, scalped her, shot her with arrows, and rode their horse over her.

She survived for several days but eventually succumbed and was interred in Weatherford's Willow Springs Cemetery, because she had asked to be buried near a church. News of her death created such a wave of outrage that Governor Sam Houston sent troops and Texas Rangers to settle the score. The scout for the mission was a young rancher named Charlie Goodnight.

Some seventy-five years after Haley recorded the story of Mrs. Sherman's death, S. C. Gwynne wrote a book on the Comanches, *Empire of the Summer Moon*, and devoted several pages to the incident. He claimed that Ezra Sherman was a "greenhorn" who didn't own a gun. Some contemporary reports said that Ezra had recently traded his rifle for an ox yoke, but the result was the same: when the Comanches showed up, the family had no defense.

"Though Martha Sherman was undoubtedly a well-intentioned and God-fearing woman, she and Ezra were part of that clamorous, chaotic, and brazenly aggressive lunge into the enemy's territory." The Shermans and the Comanches "coveted the same land," and Martha got caught in the middle (Gwynne 2010, 156–57). Gwynne included a gruesome detail I haven't seen in other accounts: Martha was gang-raped by the Comanches.

My time at Grandmother Curry's house in Seminole turned out to be more important than I ever would have imagined. It connected me to my Texas past, though I didn't realize it until years later. In 2005 I wrote a book about my mother's family, *Prairie Gothic*, and devoted two chapters to this rather famous incident in Texas history, which involved Charles Goodnight, Sam Houston, Sul Ross, Quanah Parker, and Cynthia Ann Parker, as well as poor Martha.

In 1973, I met J. Evetts Haley and will say more about him in chapter 16.

EASTWARD

In September 1966, I caught a Braniff flight out of Amarillo and flew to Dallas, then to Boston. In Cambridge, I shared a third-floor apartment near Porter Square with another Rockefeller fellow, John Lord, an affable young man from Kansas. I bought a Raleigh bicycle and rode it to campus most days. On snowy days, I caught the bus at Porter Square.

Harvard College was founded in 1636 as a training ground for Puritan ministers, and the divinity school opened as a separate institution in 1816, a nonsectarian entity with an unofficial association with the Unitarian church. Ralph Waldo Emerson studied there, as did Horatio Alger. My impression of the school in 1966 was that it produced more professors and bishops than parish ministers.

I found a bewildering variety of students. Members of my class included a Mennonite from Indiana, several Southern Baptists, a Jew from New York, four Catholics whose antiwar activities had gotten them expelled from St. John's Seminary, a student radical from California, a middle-aged man from Iran (he called it Persia), an Episcopalian who went on to become the bishop of Pennsylvania, several Lutherans from Minnesota, and a mix of Methodists, Presbyterians, and members of the United Church of Christ. A teaching assistant in one of my classes was a Seventh-day Adventist from Australia and another was a Christian from Japan.

There was even a graduate student from Abilene Christian University, a very conservative Church of Christ school in Texas. At that time, members of that denomination were just beginning to speak to Southern Baptists, never mind Catholics and Episcopalians, and I couldn't imagine what this fellow was doing at HDS.

Years later, I figured it out. Abilene Christian sent its top Bible students to HDS to study under Frank Moore Cross, G. Ernest Wright, John Strugnell, and Helmut Koester. Strugnell was a language prodigy and chief editor of the Dead Sea Scrolls project. Koester was translating and interpreting the trove of early Christian documents discovered at Nag Hammadi, Egypt, in 1945, a library of texts that give us a glimpse at the broad range of interpretations about Jesus that existed in the first three centuries AD. Those books did not make it into the New Testament canon and were suppressed by the early church.

One of Koester's graduate students was Elaine Pagels, author of *The Gnostic Gospels*. We were at HDS at the same time, but

I never met her. Five decades later, I became very interested in the Early Christian period and discovered her books.

Harvard Divinity had some of the most respected biblical scholars in the world, but I was too ignorant to know it or to take a course under any of them.

I was now a student at Harvard University, a venerable institution of higher learning that had educated four generations of Lowells and Cabots (only one generation of Kennedys at that time), and I didn't want anyone in Cambridge to detect that I was "country." I went to the Brooks Brothers store in Boston and had myself fitted for a three-piece wool herringbone suit.

I paid the princely sum of $350 for the suit and wore it to class the next day. Walking through the Harvard Yard, I began to realize that I was overdressed. Most of the natives of this place, the undergraduates, didn't wear suits and ties. Many of them wore army surplus fatigues or clothing that might have been pulled from a trash bin. They bore scant resemblance to the portraits of the Lowells and Cabots one saw hanging in the buildings. That came as a surprise.

In my first semester, my courses included a New Testament class under the Swedish scholar Krister Stendahl, a class in theology taught by Reinhold Niebuhr's brother, H. Richard (we spent the semester studying a sleep-inducing tome by Friedrich Schleiermacher), and a course in comparative religions under Wilfred Cantwell Smith.

I took a part-time job, working as a chaplain's assistant at Peter Bent Brigham Hospital in Boston, and was one of ten HDS students who served in that capacity. Twice a week, we visited the patients assigned to us, and on Saturday mornings, we met as a group to discuss our cases with Chaplain Leach, an Irish Protestant, and the hospital's staff psychiatrist, a secular Jew.

In our staff sessions, we talked about the psychological dimensions of illness, more or less within the framework of a Christian worldview. I don't recall that we ever carried Bibles to these meetings or that the Bible came up in our discussions. That seemed odd, and there were moments when I wondered what words of comfort I could offer the South American lady in room 345 who had undergone brain surgery and might not survive.

NORMAN THOMAS

Students in the divinity school were allowed to take courses in the main university, so in the fall semester I took a course in Russian. The music and literature of pre-Soviet Russia had always fascinated me and I had some vague notions about travelling there.

In the spring, I enrolled in a course taught by prominent member of the Harvard faculty David Riesman, author of a book that was widely read and praised during the sixties, *The Lonely Crowd*. I don't remember the name of the course, but it dealt with popular culture and current events, and Dr. Riesman gave us a great deal of latitude in choosing a topic for our term paper. I decided to do my essay on Norman Thomas (1884–1968), a man who played a prominent role in American politics during the 1930s and '40s.

As a student at Princeton University, Thomas studied political science under Professor Woodrow Wilson and helped establish the Intercollegiate Socialist Society. Other members of that group included Jack London, Upton Sinclair, and Clarence Darrow. After college, Thomas edited a pacifist magazine called *The World Tomorrow*, wrote several books, and ran for president six times as the candidate for the Socialist Party.

Though Thomas's political views placed him to the left of mainstream Democrats and Republicans, he was a man of eloquence and integrity, respected by clergymen, politicians, intellectuals, and journalists. Unlike many intellectuals of the day, Thomas never had romantic illusions about Soviet communism.

My interest in Thomas centered on a little-known fact about his personal history. Both his father and grandfather were Presbyterian ministers, and in his youth, he followed the same path. After graduating from Princeton in 1908, he attended Union Theological Seminary, was ordained as a Presbyterian minister in 1911, and became the pastor of East Harlem Presbyterian Church. During World War I, he was horrified by the slaughter taking place in Europe and became a pacifist. After the war, he remained a pacifist but didn't return to parish work. He formally demitted the ministry in 1931.

I met with Professor Riesman and proposed that I write an essay on Thomas's religious views, centering on why he had left the ministry and how he viewed the Christian faith after his break with the church. Dr. Riesman thought it was an excellent idea and offered to write a letter to Mr. Thomas, whom he knew, and arrange for me to go down to New York for an interview. Thomas was in his nineties, lived on Long Island, and kept an office in Lower Manhattan.

Dr. Riesman wrote his letter of introduction, and I followed up with a letter of my own, describing my project and what I wanted to accomplish in the interview. Mr. Thomas wrote back: "I should be very glad to talk to you on the questions you have in mind. The difficulty is time. I operate on a narrow margin nowadays because of legal blindness, which prevents my reading, and very considerable arthritis."

On March 17, I rode the train to New York and took a cab to a nondescript building on East 19th Street. In an office on the second floor, a male secretary worked at a typewriter and answered the phone. He told me that Mr. Thomas was busy at the moment, so I sat down, tested my tape recorder, and waited. Several minutes later, Mr. Thomas emerged from the back office, assisted by a young aide.

He was taller than I had expected (probably over six feet) and wore a well-tailored three-piece suit. A quick description of him would have included the words "patrician," "dignified," and "distant." If I had seen him on the street, I might have guessed that he was a retired Wall Street lawyer, not the most prominent American socialist since Eugene V. Debs. I couldn't help thinking, "What kind of socialist has a degree from Princeton, wears a vested suit, lives on Long Island, and keeps an office in high-rent Manhattan?"

As he drew closer, the aide whispered something, and Mr. Thomas extended his hand and waited for me to take it (he couldn't see me). I introduced myself, the aide helped him into a chair, and I began the interview, which lasted more than an hour.

Mr. Thomas concluded the session by saying, "I feel myself in many ways the weaker for lack of the kind of faith that I once had. If I were a young man today, I would not be studying for the ministry, and I am rather sorry to say that. We live in a world so mad, we have to choose between relative forms of madness. I'm sorry I couldn't have given you a better interview, but this is the way I see religion now."

The teaching assistant for my section of Dr. Riesman's class, Craig Eisendrath, gave me an A-plus on the paper.

THE ANTIWAR MOVEMENT

By the spring semester of my first year, the sentiment against the war in Vietnam had become a major distraction to me and many of my fellow students. Although several of my friends in Texas considered it their patriotic duty to support the war,

I thought the Johnson administration had failed, miserably, to give the American people a compelling reason why it was in our national interest to be there.

This wasn't like Pearl Harbor. We hadn't been attacked. It was a conflict created by officials in the State Department who were playing geopolitical chess, hoping to contain communism in a country ten thousand miles away. It was supposed to be a "little war" that we could control, but it got out of hand. It was a war we shouldn't have entered and couldn't win—and didn't. We lost and paid a terrible price: fifty thousand dead, thousands maimed, and a country left angry and divided through the final quarter of the twentieth century.

When HDS students gathered after class, we didn't discuss theology or biblical scholarship. We talked about our obligation to oppose a war that we considered unjust, unnecessary, and immoral. It became almost an obsession, driven in part by guilt. As ministerial students, we were exempted from the draft and classified 4-D.

Many of us became active in a group that had sprung up on the East Coast, Clergy and Laymen Concerned about Vietnam. I think it might have originated at Yale Divinity School. At any rate, Yale's chaplain, William Sloane Coffin Jr., served as its loudest and most visible spokesman.

In March, I joined a group of HDS students who drove to Washington to attend a large rally of pastors, priests, rabbis, and seminarians. We heard speeches by Reverend Coffin, Philip and Daniel Berrigan (they were brothers and Catholic priests), and Rabbi Abraham Heschel.* After the sessions, seminarians talked about civil disobedience, burning draft cards, and moving to Canada.

* Twenty years later, Father Daniel Berrigan played the part of a Jesuit priest in the movie *The Mission*.

In April, we held our own conference at HDS, inviting divinity students from Harvard, Yale, Union, Andover-Newton, Princeton, and Episcopal Theological Seminary. Notably absent were Catholic seminarians. Cardinal Cushing of Boston, a friend of the Kennedy family, supported the war and had clamped a lid on anti-Vietnam protests.

Our main speaker for the conference was HDS professor Harvey Cox, whose popular book *The Secular City* had made him *Time* magazine's go-to guy when they needed a quote from a theologian. Since I was taking a course under Professor Cox that semester and had struck up a slight acquaintance with him, I gave his introduction at the conference.

Professor Cox was one of the first HDS faculty members to speak out in public against the war. Some of the faculty tried to conduct business as usual and avoid the topic of Vietnam, but it was like throwing sandbags against a rising river. The campus had been swept up in the rebellion of the sixties, and for many of us in the divinity school, social issues became the only moral absolutes in a world turned upside down.

CHAPTER 5

BOSTON 1967–68

When I left Texas in the fall of 1966 and went off to divinity school, I had been dating Kris for nine months and we had grown very fond of each other. Even so, neither of us felt ready to make a commitment to marriage and decided that it would be wise to test our feelings against time and distance.

I was single my first year at Harvard but never went out on a date. Old movie revivals had become a popular form of entertainment around Harvard Square, and a Texas friend and I spent our Saturday nights watching the black-and-white films of Laurel and Hardy, Humphrey Bogart, the Marx Brothers, and Charlie Chaplin.

Kris and I carried on a regular exchange of letters, and a big chunk of my Rockefeller fellowship was diverted into paying for long-distance phone calls. Over the Christmas break, I flew back to Dallas and asked her if she would marry me.

At UT when I asked (or at least thought I was asking) for her phone number, she had given me a playful, evasive reply. This time, she said, "YES!" It was the best, luckiest day of my life. I was proud but scared silly. I had no idea how I would support us.

We married in Dallas in August 1967 and made the long drive to Boston in a new Volkswagen station wagon my parents had given us as a wedding gift. We pulled a small U-Haul trailer packed with wedding gifts, books, clothes, and my Gretsch 5-string banjo.

We also had a record player and several boxes of LP records that we had acquired during our undergraduate days. Conspicuously absent were albums by pop singers and rock groups. Somehow Kris and I missed out on that part of the 1960s. Neither of us attended rock concerts or developed much interest in the groups that were popular among our peers, even The Rolling Stones and The Beatles.

The music of The Beatles struck me as noisy and juvenile until they brought out *Sgt. Pepper's Lonely Hearts Club Band*, and that got my attention. All at once, they were making serious music. I never developed any interest in The Stones. I couldn't see past Mick Jagger, who struck me as a sneering little hedonist with an exceptionally ugly mouth. Just looking at him destroyed my desire to hear anything he might call music.

My record collection fell into three main categories: classical, choral, and folk. The folk artists I admired included The Weavers, Pete Seeger, Erik Darling, Odetta, Joan Baez, Judy Collins, Bob Dylan, and Miriam Makeba. My favorite classical composer at that time was Ralph Vaughan Williams, and I owned a number of his symphonies. My choral records included requiem masses, sacred numbers from the Renaissance, and Gregorian chant.

When we reached Boston, we shopped around for an apartment and chose one on Park Drive in Boston's Fenway District.

I had to commute across the river to the divinity school in Cambridge, but the apartment was close to Kris's job with an insurance company in downtown Boston. The place was small but nice and cost more than we had hoped to pay. It consisted of a tiny kitchen, a living room with a bay window, and a small bedroom. On game days, we could hear the cheers and groans of Red Sox fans at Fenway Park.

We had no furniture, so I bought tools and paint, made a dining table out of a wooden cable spool, and built four stools out of lumber. We scrounged a decent used carpet for the living room, and our bed consisted of a piece of three-inch foam rubber laid on the floor. During the day, we added pillows and a cloth cover that Kris had made with her sewing machine, and it served as a sofa.

We slept in the living room so that I could use the bedroom as a study. We made bookshelves out of cinder blocks and 1x8 pine boards, and I cobbled up a "desk" out of a hollow-core door laid between two stacks of boxes. On the desk, I kept typing paper, carbon paper, a dictionary, and my old faithful Smith-Corona portable electric typewriter. My parents had given it to me as a high school graduation present, and I ran miles of paper through it.

The fact that we had sacrificed a substantial part of our living space to provide me with a study revealed an important change in my thinking. I had made the decision to start writing every day, first thing in the morning. Professional writers have professional habits. They write every day and don't wait for inspiration.

Kris supported me in this effort and gave up her bedroom so that I could do it. Had she not encouraged me to do something with my talent, I doubt that I would have gone to the trouble. And it *was* a lot of trouble. As a single man, I had been a carefree night owl. Now, I had to change all my patterns and rhythms.

Kris's presence in my life forced me to reach beyond myself, "and in the process of trying to conceal from her what I actually was, I became what I should have been" (Erickson 2009, 11).

A WRITING CLASS

I began writing every morning and enrolled in a course that was offered at Harvard College, Professor Theodore Morrison's two-semester class on fiction writing. It was one of those courses that had a reputation on campus, along with those taught by Henry Kissinger, John Kenneth Galbraith, B. F. Skinner, and David Riesman. Norman Mailer and John Updike had taken Professor Morrison's course when they were undergraduates.

Getting into the class wasn't easy. Professor Morrison limited the enrollment to fifteen students, and they had to submit a sample of their writing. You got into the course only if he thought you had some potential as a writer. I found this rather intimidating, competing for a spot against kids who had gone to prep schools and come to Harvard laboring under the weight of their academic honors. I don't remember what I submitted as a writing sample, but Professor Morrison must have thought it showed promise and allowed me into his class.

We met twice a week in Warren House, not far from Widener Library. We sat around a long hardwood table, surrounded by walls of rich hardwood paneling—the real thing, not a cheap veneer imitation. We could almost sense the presence of Mailer and Updike in the room, scowling down at us and wondering if we really deserved to be there.

Professor Morrison had grown up in New England and graduated from Harvard. At sixty-six, he was handsome and dignified, with a mane of white hair, alabaster skin, liquid blue eyes, and delicate hands. He came to class in a tweed sports jacket, V-neck sweater, and tie. He was quiet, gentle, and always pleasant, but reserved.

He was also modest. I don't recall his talking much about his own writing career or accomplishments, although he did mention that he had known Robert Frost.

When Morrison died in 1988, the *New York Times* thought enough of him to publish his obituary, listing him as "Poet and Professor" (November 29, 1988). The memorial noted that in addition to teaching at Harvard, he had served as associate editor of *Atlantic Monthly* and as director of the Bread Loaf Writers' Conference and had published five novels and several volumes of poetry.

His approach to teaching was very casual. He didn't lecture, give tests, or assign homework. We students wrote stories and he read them aloud to the class, then we discussed them while he listened and puffed on his pipe. Sometimes he injected a comment, but mostly we were critiquing our own work—the blind leading the ignorant, I thought on several occasions.

TOM MCMAHON

I didn't get acquainted with the students in the class, most of whom were undergraduates at Harvard College or Radcliffe. I was married, lived across the river in Boston, worked an evening job, and wasn't a part of their world. They all appeared to be what you would expect: bright and talented.

The most promising writer in the class was a tall, quiet fellow named Tom McMahon. He usually came to class wearing a jacket and tie and said hardly a word to anyone. He was working on a doctorate at MIT and had gotten special permission to attend the class.

While the rest of us struggled with short stories, Tom had finished the first draft of a novel. He brought chapters to class, pages typed on yellow paper and secured with a paper clip. I think he had already gotten some editorial help from Professor Morrison before he enrolled in the course.

His novel dealt with the experiences of Timmy, a boy growing up in Los Alamos, New Mexico, during World War II, when its citizens included J. Robert Oppenheimer, Richard Feynman, and other scientists who were developing the atomic bomb. McMahon wrote well—solid sentences, vivid characters, and descriptions that seemed almost photographic in their detail—and made good use of his background in science. When he wrote about physics and physicists, he knew what he was talking about.

When Professor Morrison read McMahon's chapters aloud to the class, we didn't need to ask what he thought. It showed on his face. The teacher was proud of the student, and there was no doubt that, as a writer, McMahon was far more advanced than the rest of us.

But I couldn't help noticing the air of darkness that hung over his story. As we learned more about Timmy, we began to realize that he was struggling with mental illness. McMahon used the metaphor of mental illness to describe life in the Atomic Age.

The novels of the late sixties—the fiction we were trying to imitate—often had a dark quality and every one of us in that class wrote gloomy stories, stories that contained no joy or laughter. Gloom just seemed to be in the air, permeating our fiction and taken as a sign of intellectual depth, even a badge of honor. If you weren't depressed about something, how smart could you be?

Years later, I found myself wondering how someone from another epoch, another country, or another culture might have viewed us. He might have asked, "What's so depressing about attending an elite university, eating three meals a day, sleeping in a warm bed, and spending hours every day reading the great works of Western civilization in Widener Library, one of the great libraries of the civilized world?"

It seemed to be an affliction unique to the academic arena and it persists to this day. I cured myself by leaving the university environment, but it has continued to puzzle me. We were sheltered from hunger, disease, crime, and even the war in Southeast Asia . . . and we were depressed about it?

There might be a complex explanation, but I prefer a simple one. People who don't believe the first sentence of the first book of the Bible tend to find life depressing. They write novels about life and teach those novels in college classes and produce new generations of novelists who are privileged and depressed, and the beat goes on.

But back to Tom McMahon. A year later, he found a publisher for his novel—Little, Brown and Company of Boston, probably with help from Professor Morrison—and it came out in 1970 under the title *Principles of American Nuclear Chemistry: A Novel.* The dedication said, "To Theodore Morrison."

I was sad to learn that Tom McMahon died in 1999 at the age of 55 of complications following surgery. He had been a professor in the science department at Harvard and had published several novels. A story in the *Harvard University Gazette* (February 18, 1999) read, "Throughout his life, McMahon successfully united science and literature, using the imaginative resources of one world to enrich his work in the other."

I can't say that I learned much about writing in Professor Morrison's class, but it did serve an important function, giving me a reason to establish the discipline of writing every morning. And, for the first time, I began thinking about writing a novel. Tom McMahon had written one. Maybe I could too.

NIGHT JOB

I attended classes during the day and worked evenings for an executive search company in Waltham. There, I spent four hours per shift on the phone cold-calling engineers and scientists in the aerospace/defense industry to see if they might be interested in checking around for a better position at companies such as Raytheon, General Dynamics, and LTV. They seemed to be a restless group, always looking for a better deal.

Paul, the owner of the company, was an Irish Catholic in his forties and a business graduate of Boston College. In his office he kept framed pictures of his pretty wife and three smiling children, and he told me that he taught a Sunday school class. He had a muscular build, a generous head of hair, and a suave presence on the telephone. He cut a handsome figure in his expensive suits and starched white shirts.

Like all the Boston Irish I met, he had no love for Harvard. When he said the word "Harvard," my Southern ears heard it as "Have It." Even so, he hired Harvard seminarians to work for his company, figuring they were likely to be literate, competent, and honest.

Paul usually left the office before I arrived, but one evening he stayed late, and after I had finished my conversation with an engineer in New Hampshire, he called me into his office. He had removed his suit jacket and wore a spotless white shirt and expensive tie and was engulfed in a huge executive chair, surrounded by pictures of his family. We talked for a while, then he picked up the phone and dialed a number.

When the other party answered, he smiled and began speaking in a low, confidential tone, as though he were alone in the room. He and the other party talked for fifteen or twenty minutes and arranged to meet somewhere. I soon realized that he was arranging a tryst with a woman who wasn't the mother of his happy children. I didn't want to listen but had no choice.

He hung up the phone and gave me a man-to-man smirk but never explained how it all fit together: business ethics, marriage vows, children, Sunday school, and a mistress on the side.

MUGGED BY NIETZSCHE

In the spring of 1968, I took a course in theology under a respected member of the faculty. At the end of the semester, he asked us to choose a theologian or philosopher and to write a critical essay on his view of Christianity. I chose Friedrich Nietzsche because I admired his writing style. He wrote beautiful, lucid prose.

My scuffles with other German thinkers had not turned out well. Some of the darkest hours of my university experience had come when I was hunched over a tome by Hegel, Kant, or Schleiermacher, twisting a strand of hair and muttering, "What are you talking about!"

I wasn't well suited to the discipline of philosophy. I had an artistic temperament and so did Nietzsche. I knew that he was a vociferous atheist and an enemy of the church, but I rather enjoyed watching him throw jabs in the face of flabby bourgeois Christianity. I figured it might be fun to spar a few rounds with him in my term paper.

I didn't expect to get mugged, but that's how it turned out. I submitted my essay and made an appointment with the professor to discuss it. I told him, "Nietzsche won. I couldn't answer his arguments."

When you make such a statement to a prominent theologian, in an institution that claims to be Christian, you should expect a stern response. I had come to the meeting prepared to receive a verbal lashing. There was no lashing, no thunder or lightning, no outrage, no suggestion that I had missed the whole point of the assignment. Instead, the professor gave me a reading list and sent me on my way with an A-minus. I suppose he admired my skill at covering intellectual emptiness with clever prose.

When I look back on my fascination with Nietzsche, I'm embarrassed. I would rather not remember that I swooned over a pagan thinker whose writings released the germs of nihilism, but to be fair, I wasn't alone. Students of my generation were in a rebellious mood and prone to listen to anyone who flagged the outrages of Christian armies, tyrants, popes, inquisitors, and executioners.

We had gone blind to the riches we had inherited from Christian civilization and took them for granted. A short list would include freedom of the individual, the value and dignity of human life, romantic love, limited government, the protection of children, and rights for women. Science developed in the Christian West, and so did the idea of universal education.

In my term paper, I missed those details.

Those of us involved in the antiwar movement often invoked the Just War Doctrine in our protest documents but gave little thought to where it originated: Augustine of Hippo, a church bishop. Before Augustine, educated, enlightened human beings accepted the view that a war should consist of unlimited slaughter and looting, and should include the enslavement of anyone who could perform labor. The Just War Doctrine brought an entirely new way of viewing warfare, and *it was a Christian idea.* The leaders of "civilized" Rome despised it.

The anti-slavery movements in England and America introduced another uniquely Christian idea to the world. Before Christians raised their voices, slavery had been accepted as good and normal in virtually every country on Earth, including those in Africa where Euro-American slavery began, with black

Africans selling black Africans to Arab traders. In the American South, preachers and theologians defended slavery as biblical, but Christians in other places objected, supported anti-slavery laws, and laid the foundation for the American Civil Rights Movement of the sixties.

As students, we heaped harsh judgment on the Christian West, but rarely wondered, "Compared to what?" The "what" was always some form of utopian ideal. But utopian ideals hadn't done so well either. In the twentieth century, secular utopian idealists presided over the extermination of a hundred million people, all killed for some kind of "higher good." History had never produced a more efficient set of butchers.

In my term paper, I missed that detail.

I also overlooked that Nietzsche's godless worldview didn't account for the wonders of creation, the absolute miracles that occur in front of us every minute of every day: that eyes can see and ears can hear; that birds fly south in the fall and homely caterpillars transform themselves into lovely butterflies; that humans, composed of trillions of individual cells, can walk upright on two legs, read books, fall in love, and write poetry; and that sometime around AD 1800, two microscopic, mute, blind, deaf cells converged and became the man who delivered the Gettysburg Address.

Nietzsche's atheism couldn't explain how or why any of this occurred—indeed, why *anything* had ever occurred. Without a design and a designer, nothing should have happened. The universe should be filled with inert particles that have no reason to move or combine or do anything. We should have nothingness doing nothing.

Nietzsche gave no satisfactory answers to the most important questions a human being can ask: Who am I? Where did I come from? Why am I here? What am I supposed to be doing on this earth, and what becomes of me when I die?

I could have mentioned that in my term paper but didn't.

I was a dilettante and that gave me some excuse, but what about my professor? He had a doctorate from Yale Divinity School and was being paid to guide the unenlightened. If he had answers to Nietzsche, why didn't he share them with me?

He gave me a reading list that didn't mention any books by Francis Schaeffer or John Warwick Montgomery, both of whom were writing solid defenses of orthodox Christianity. Any well-read, alert Christian scholar should have known their work. He should have demanded that I read C. S. Lewis, but Lewis wasn't on the list either. If Nietzsche was an intellectual giant, so was Lewis. After spending his youth in the embrace of the fashionable atheism of his day, the latter emerged with a clear, resounding defense of the Christian faith. He wrote strong, vivid prose that any dilettante could understand and admire. He even had a sense of humor.

Best of all, at the end of his life, Lewis wasn't insane. Nietzsche most certainly was.

Maybe my professor was having a bad day. Maybe he was tired of trying to teach mouthy students who thought they already knew everything. But he shouldn't have allowed me to walk out of his office thinking that Nietzsche had obliterated nineteen hundred years of Christian intellectual and moral accomplishment. He should have said something like this: "Nietzsche was a brilliant, tormented genius who gave us the blueprint for spiritual disintegration and Hell on Earth. He beat you up because you're weak, rebellious, and ignorant. Worse, you're proud of it. Take your paper and write it again. You're not nearly as smart as you think you are—and in case you haven't figured it out yet, *neither was Nietzsche*."

CHAPTER 6

BACK TO TEXAS

At the end of the 1968 spring semester, I wasn't sure what direction I wanted to take in finding a career, but the parish ministry didn't seem a likely prospect. Theology just wasn't my natural language.

I explored the idea of combining my interests in literature and theology and applied to several graduate schools that had programs of that nature: Emory and the University of Chicago, as I recall. Bless them, they both turned me down. It stung my pride but spared me and them a lot of misery. I didn't belong in the academic world, but it took me a while to figure that out.

I decided to take a year's leave of absence from the divinity school, do some writing, and think about the future. We weren't sure exactly where we were going to move or what I would do to make a living, but we felt it was time to move back to Texas. Austin seemed a good destination. As they used to say, "Everyone moves back to Austin." We began packing our things.

It happened that my cousin Mike Harter was traveling around the East Coast at the time. He stayed with us for several days and helped with the loading up. In our Boston apartment, Kris packed boxes with loving care and labeled each with a marker, while Mike and I played chess and listened to the music of Bob Dylan, whom we had just discovered. (Within months, Mike had bought a guitar and harmonica and was singing Dylan songs better than Bob.) When Kris finished filling and labeling the boxes, Mike and I lugged them down two flights of stairs and fitted them into a six-foot U-Haul trailer.

Mike and I were born a month apart and were babies together during World War II. While our fathers served in the Pacific Theater, our mothers lived with their parents in Seminole, Texas. Mike's mother, Aunt Bennett, had married a German Catholic, so Mike was raised in the Catholic Church and attended elementary school at St. Elizabeth's in Lubbock.

During the fifties, Catholics and Baptists weren't on the friendliest of terms, and there was wariness and suspicion on both sides. In Perryton and Lubbock, the uneasiness never burst out into the open or became ugly, but it was there, simmering below the surface. Some sharp edges appeared during the presidential election of 1960. When John F. Kennedy won the presidency, there were people in my hometown who braced themselves for an invasion of Jesuits and nuns.

Even so, Cousin Mike and I had a pleasant ecumenical boyhood. When we came together at family functions, he said his prayers in Latin and I said mine in Baptist King James Bible English. We knew nothing about the long and bloody conflicts between Protestants and Catholics in the old country. In our little world, God spoke both Latin and English, and it wasn't a big deal.

While I was a student at HDS, Mike was studying theology at Conception Seminary in Missouri, and we carried on a lively exchange of letters about a couple of trendy books that were getting a lot of attention on our campuses.

Joseph Fletcher, a professor at Episcopal Theological Seminary, had come out with a book called *Situation Ethics*. I didn't read it myself (I was slogging through Friedrich Schleiermacher), but many students did, and their reports suggested that Dr. Fletcher had produced an intellectual tour de force. He had succeeded in putting a scholarly gloss on an idea that, for centuries, had been regarded as mere adolescent fantasy: "Make up the rules as you go along and call it Christian!"

The other book was Thomas J. J. Altizer's *Radical Theology and the Death of God*. *Time* magazine had taken Altizer's thoughts into middle-class living rooms with a cover story that screeched, "IS GOD DEAD?" Altizer, a professor of "religion" at Emory University, said yes, God was dead, but in Jesus we had a nice little guy who had set a good example for mankind, and that should be enough to keep Christianity chugging along.

Mike and I had embraced liberalism and heaped our share of criticism on the church, but *this*? It struck us as something that might have begun as a prank at *Mad* magazine, yet thoughtful, educated Christians—Protestants and Catholics—were reading the books and talking about them in solemn tones.

The God Is Dead school of "theology" had taken liberal Christianity beyond satire and to the outer limits of the solar system. At that point, we either turned around and headed back home or went spiraling off into a great cackling darkness.

HORSEMAN IN A FOG

Over the years, people have asked, "What was it like, being at Harvard?" It's an obvious question: Country boy goes off to one of the world's most renowned universities and . . . well?

I still don't have a clear, simple answer. In conversations about my college years, I seldom mention Harvard by name. It's such a powerful brand, it creates false notions and expectations:

> If you went there, you must have been brilliant.
> It must have been a life-changing experience.

I don't consider either of those statements to be correct. My two years on campus informed me that a small-town Texas kid could compete in such a place and, for me, that was important information. I could scratch it off my list of things to worry about.

After I left Harvard, I never went back. For more than fifty years, I received and ignored invitations to join the Harvard Club of Dallas. I felt honored to have been a part of that community for two years, but whatever Harvard was or meant or signified, I didn't absorb it.

It was as though I had spent two years prowling around a world-famous museum, looking at all the exhibits and taking notes. I had gone there thinking that I would become a part of that world, only to discover that it wasn't possible. I sometimes think that both the school and I would have been better off if I had spent those two years herding cattle in the Davis Mountains and reading the Great Books at night.

It turned out that a church-related vocation wasn't for me, but I did give it serious consideration, and my time at HDS provided some balance to the secular education I had acquired at UT. My main regret is that I didn't take any Bible courses under Frank Moore Cross, G. Ernest Wright, Helmut Koester, or John Strugnell. They were world-class scholars, but I wasn't astute enough to know it. Sigh.

I'm sure the times had a lot to do with it. The years I spent at HDS were among the most tumultuous in American history.

The tectonic plates of national thought and tradition had begun to shift under the strains of racial unrest, the Vietnam War, scientific discoveries, technology, the sexual revolution, and who knows what else. During those two years, the foundations trembled.

George Will called 1968 "perhaps the worst year in American history." Martin Luther King and Bobby Kennedy fell to assassins' bullets, cities were exploding in riots, and the entire country was in an uproar about the war in Vietnam. Our nation seemed to be coming apart at the seams.

For one reason or another, Harvard and I passed each other like horsemen in a fog. If I had been there in calmer times, who knows, the story might have had a different ending. I'm glad things turned out the way they did. I found my way back home.

PART 2

THE CIVIL RIGHTS MOVEMENT

CHAPTER 7

MISSISSIPPI AND NEW YORK

It seems strange that a kid from Perryton, Texas, got swept up in the Civil Rights Movement, but I did.

Residents of my hometown had little exposure to people with dark skin and African features. There were none living there. When our football teams played Borger and Pampa, we encountered Black athletes, and when my family made trips to Amarillo, we saw Black people on the streets and in the stores. We never met them, and they were objects of curiosity.

Some of my ancestors were Quakers who opposed slavery. Others served in the Confederate Army, but they didn't have a strong emotional stake in slavery or in the laws of racial separation that followed the Civil War. To them, the Civil War was a response to Yankee aggression, not a defense of slavery.

The members of my family had little to say about Black people, one way or another. When they did, they didn't use racial slurs and were sympathetic to the arguments against segregation.

It was during my junior year in high school when I began hearing about the racial unrest in the Southern states, probably starting with the integration of Central High School in Little Rock. I had a curious mind and had begun reading about Darwin, Freud, French poets, and segregation in the South. My Sunday school teacher wasn't a reader or a thinker and wasn't pleased when I pressed him with questions about evolution and racial injustice.

The answer always seemed to be, "Good Baptists don't ask those questions." That didn't satisfy me. The Southern Baptist Church—the largest Protestant denomination in the United States, with hundreds of millions of dollars' worth of church real estate and thousands of preachers and theologians on the payroll—should have prepared an intelligent rebuttal to Darwinism and should have taken a stand against Jim Crow laws and segregation, but they hadn't done it.

Or so it seemed to me at the wise old age of seventeen.

To me and many other young people who were coming of age in the early sixties, it appeared that Christians were talking only to themselves and were sending their children off to college poorly prepared to defend their faith against students and professors who considered the Bible a book of fairy tales. Off we went, like rabbits hopping toward a canyon bristling with hungry coyotes.

Over in England, C. S. Lewis had spent three decades defending the faith with arguments that were razor-sharp, meeting the critics on their own ground and thrashing them with logic and biting humor. But Lewis was an Anglican living in England, not a Baptist in Texas, and we didn't know about him.

I moved away from the church, feeling angry and disappointed, but today, I look back and wonder: *What could the Baptists have said or done that would have satisfied me?* If my Sunday school teacher had used Lewis's *Mere Christianity* as a text, I probably wouldn't have read it, or if I had read it, I might not have had the intellectual maturity to understand it.

I was rebellious and lazy, and we can't blame that on the church. Rebellion was in the air. I remember the first rock-and-roll song I ever heard, "Rock Around the Clock" by Bill Haley & His Comets. It appeared in a grim black-and-white movie called *Blackboard Jungle* about a white teacher in an all-Black high school in New York City. I saw it in Perryton's Ellis Theater, and it must have been in the late 1950s. When the song began, high school kids in the audience burst into cheers and clapping. I had never seen anything quite like it. It was as though someone had opened dusty drapes and let the sunshine in.

The song seemed to touch a hidden nerve that had been put to sleep during the fifties, a time of stability and conformity when almost everybody went to church, boys got a haircut every two weeks, and almost everyone wanted to be "normal" and middle class, get a good job, and buy a house in the suburbs.

Although the words of the song could hardly have been more banal, there must have been something in the beat or the presentation that suggested rebellion, and it split the audience in the theater right down the middle. The teenagers cheered; the adults shook their heads in dismay. A few years later, Bob Dylan captured the mood in "The Times They Are A-Changin'."

Indeed they were. The surface tranquility of the fifties concealed powerful currents that were pulling us toward the waterfall of the sixties. It changed everyone and everything.

In 1961, my brother Charles was studying at the University of Texas and had gotten involved with a group of students and faculty who rallied around Ronnie Dugger's liberal biweekly newspaper, *The Texas Observer*. Three of UT's best-known professors—John Silber, Roger Shattuck, and William Arrowsmith—contributed articles to the paper, as did a young Rhodes Scholar from Mississippi, Willie Morris. Their articles helped create the impression that "liberal" and "intelligent" were synonyms.

On a visit to Austin that year, I joined my brother and his friends in a picket line in front of the Varsity Theatre on Guadalupe Street, across from the UT campus. It was an exciting adventure, but more than that, it seemed right. Back at Perryton High School, I became the liberal-in-residence, arguing the case against segregation with my classmates and backing up my arguments with articles from *The Texas Observer*.

MISSISSIPPI

In my first year of college at the University of Denver, I went out of my way to make the acquaintance of Black people, the first I had ever met. I wanted to learn more about them. Paul Hamilton from Pueblo, Colorado, became a good friend, and so did a tall, willowy young lady from Brooklyn. She and my pal Mickey Edstrom began dating and later married, even though she told me that her father didn't like white people.

During the spring break in 1963, the University YMCA sponsored a project to send three carloads of students to study conditions in the state of Mississippi, which had gotten considerable media attention for its harsh segregation laws. We were proud to advertise ourselves as an integrated group: nine white students, one white faculty advisor, two Black coeds, and an African graduate student named Selby Hlatchwayo.

We understood, in a vague, inexperienced manner, that there was a certain element of danger in this project, but Mississippi was more dangerous than we knew. The people who ran things were very serious about separating the races and they had the full power of the state to enforce their laws. In 1963, Mississippi was a world unto itself.

Today, I'm surprised that the people in charge of the university YMCA agreed to sponsor the trip, and that the school administration allowed it to proceed. My father, who read *Time* magazine every week and kept up with the national news, raised strong objections and urged me against the venture. But those were heady times, and we were bubbling with optimism and the rightness of our cause. I was determined to go and sold my gun collection to pay for the trip.

To record the events on our expedition, I carried a small Kodak camera and a hardbound journal book. The journal got lost during one of the many moves I made later in my college days, so I have to rely on a time-dimmed memory, with some help from the internet. My color slides of the trip survived until 2017, when our ranch house burned in a wildfire.

Off we went to the vine-covered darkness that was Mississippi during the governorship of Ross Barnett. We spent our first night at Wiley College, a small Black school in Marshall, Texas, then pushed on to Mississippi, where we stayed at Millsaps College in Jackson.

Our main contact in Mississippi was John Salter, an instructor at all-Black Tougaloo College. It is worth noting that the University of Denver, Wiley, Millsaps, and Tougaloo were all affiliated with Protestant denominations. They were not secular state-supported institutions.

I remember John Salter as young, vigorous, handsome, and full of bright energy. He dressed in blue-collar clothes and had worked as a labor organizer before moving to Mississippi to get involved in the civil rights movement. He served on the executive board of the Jackson NAACP.

Millsaps College was not an integrated school but had become a place where pioneers of the civil rights movement, both Blacks and whites, could meet and talk. While we were there, we met several Black students who had come over from Tougaloo College. They considered Millsaps a safe location, but it wasn't as safe as they might have supposed. Salter knew he was being watched by agents of the powerful White Citizens' Councils.

One night I stayed up late, talking to one of the Tougaloo students who had grown up in the Delta town of Greenwood, Mississippi. In a quiet voice, he told me about the murder of Emmett Till, a chilling memory from his childhood that occurred in the little town of Money, eight miles north of Greenwood.

At that time, the story was not well known outside of Mississippi, but in years to come, I heard it many times. For allegedly insulting a married white woman, Emmett Till was kidnapped, beaten, and shot, his body tied with weights and dumped into the Tallahatchie River. The two white men charged with the murder were acquitted by an all-white jury that deliberated only sixty-seven minutes. One of the jurors told the press that they would have reached a verdict sooner, only they paused for a soda pop break.

John Salter arranged for us to meet a journalist named Hodding Carter, whose small-town newspaper, the Greenville *Democrat-Times*, had taken a strong stand against racial intolerance. Carter had written a blistering editorial about the Emmett Till case and an article for *Look* magazine about the White Citizens' Council in Mississippi.

Outside the Deep South, Carter was often praised as "the spokesman for the New South," but his article in *Look* magazine drew a loud rebuke from the Mississippi legislature. (Carter's son, Hodding Carter III, served in the Jimmy Carter administration as spokesman for the State Department.)

MEDGAR EVERS AND ROSS BARNETT

John Salter arranged for our group to spend a morning with one of his colleagues, the field secretary of the NAACP in Jackson, Medgar Evers. Evers had grown up in rural Mississippi, served as an army sergeant in WWII, played football at Alcorn College, earned a degree in business, and sold insurance before getting involved in the civil rights movement.

It was impossible not to admire Evers. He came across as warm, likeable, intelligent, handsome, modest, determined, and courageous. He had steel in his eyes, and in his line of work, he needed it. He lived in a dangerous world and had received threats on his life. The day we were there, he showed us several fresh bullet holes in the front window of the NAACP headquarters.

Our group spent the afternoon walking around downtown Jackson and took pleasure in "integrating" the state Capitol Building, which still had separate bathrooms and drinking fountains for whites and "coloreds." Then we paid a visit to the headquarters of the White Citizens' Council near the Capitol Building. They had been tipped off that we were coming, and their response to us was cordial but wary.

We even had a thirty-minute audience with Governor Barnett himself. Up close, the governor could hardly have seemed more benign: a successful lawyer who had made a considerable amount of money arguing damage suits; a popular politician who spoke with pride about his efforts to bring new industry to the state; a grandfather wearing spectacles and a nice suit, who probably dyed his hair to cover the gray; a modest, humorless gentleman who spoke in the slow, word-stretching accent of the rural South.

He was also the most powerful political figure in a state whose laws demanded that Medgar Evers, a college graduate and a veteran of the United States Army, ride in the back of a bus.

To those of us from the outside, Mississippi's system of racial separation seemed backward, corrupt, self-crippling, and just *wrong*. Meeting Governor Barnett and Medgar Evers on the same day, in the same city, in the same dimension of time, did nothing to enhance our understanding.

Five decades later, that same puzzle about Mississippi found expression in the movie *The Help*, whose story occurred around the time I was there. It mentioned both Medgar Evers and Ross Barnett.

Governor Barnett gave no indication that he objected to our presence in his domain, but as we were leaving the Capitol grounds and walking down the street, a police car pulled up and two men came over and began asking questions. One wore a police uniform and the second did not. He might have been a plainclothes detective or a representative from the White Citizens' Council.

They showed none of the governor's bland congeniality. They listened with hard eyes as our student leader, Kathy Sutton, explained what we were doing. While Kathy was talking, I realized that my little Kodak camera was hanging around my neck, pointing toward the officers. Without taking my eyes off the policemen, I eased my hand into position and groped around with my finger until I felt the shutter button. I snapped a picture of the scene, timing a cough to hide the sound.

The officers didn't hear the click of the camera, but several of my comrades did, and they were horrified. The officers let us go with a warning: "You're in Mississippi now. Don't push your luck." When the police car pulled away, my colleagues heaved a sigh of relief, then let me know that taking the photograph had been an uncommonly stupid thing to do.

They were right, of course. Ross Barnett's Mississippi was the wrong place to be practicing amateur heroics, as events of the following summer made clear.

NEW YORK CITY

Three months after this trip, I took a job as a summer intern with the East Harlem Protestant Parish. I was one of fifteen college students, most of us white and from the South, who spent the summer working in all-Black churches in the part of Manhattan known as East Harlem, located between Midtown and Central Harlem.

Every morning, I rode the subway from Methodist Hospital in Brooklyn, where our group stayed, to Jefferson Park Methodist Church on East 107th Street, in the company of two other summer interns: Trish Jarvis, a Methodist minister's daughter from West Virginia, and Naboth Mbawa, an African pre-med student at Lawrence College in Wisconsin.

Naboth and I shared a room at Methodist Hospital. He grew up in Southern Rhodesia (now Zimbabwe) and had been educated in schools run by Methodist missionaries. He spoke perfect English in the accent of his native tongue, Shona, and was extremely neat and almost compulsive about brushing his teeth. He was sullen the first hour after getting out of bed, but funny, exuberant, alert, and astute the rest of the time.

Naboth played the guitar and loved to sing. I had brought my banjo, and we often played and sang together. He was surprised that I had a collection of Miriam Makeba albums and knew some of her songs. She was a South African singer and popular in Rhodesia.

Trish, Naboth, and I assisted the pastor, John Collins, with the youth program and with what the Methodists called "vacation church school" (Southern Baptists called it "Bible school"). On weekdays, Reverend Collins wore jeans, work boots, a black shirt, and a clerical collar, and was like no preacher I had ever encountered. Loud, gruff, blunt, and divorced, he smoked cigars inside the church and didn't try to conceal his appetite for a few bottles of suds after a day's work.

He wouldn't have lasted ten minutes in any church I had attended, but he seemed a good match for his congregation. His Black parishioners were fond of him.

I met other pastors and administrators who worked with the East Harlem Protestant Parish, and they, too, struck me as rather worldly. They didn't carry Bibles or even talk much about it. It seemed that many of them had experienced a crisis of faith and had taken refuge in the civil rights movement, a moral constant in a shifting world.

In my work at the church, I took children on field trips to places of interest (the Staten Island Ferry, the Empire State Building, the Bronx Zoo, a game at Yankee Stadium) and wrote a little play that the kids performed for a gathering of parents. I don't remember anything about the play except that it dealt with a civil rights theme, and it was well received.

I'm sure Charles Wesley would have considered it Social Gospel wearing the thinnest of Christian clothes.

THE MURDER OF MEDGAR EVERS

On long subway rides from Brooklyn to our stop at 110th Street, Naboth read his *Christian Science Monitor* (he considered their coverage of Africa the best of any American newspaper) and I read about events in Mississippi in the *Times*. On June 13, I was shocked on reading that Medgar Evers had been murdered in his front yard.

He had just returned from a meeting at the NAACP and started toward the house, carrying a bundle of T-shirts bearing the message "Jim Crow Must Go," when he was struck in the back by a bullet fired from a .303 Enfield rifle. He lived for an hour and died at a hospital, probably in a wing set aside for "coloreds." He was buried at Arlington National Cemetery with full military honors, with a crowd of three thousand people attending.

The murder caused a national uproar, but police had no suspects until the following year, when a man named Byron De La Beckwith, a fertilizer salesman and member of the White Citizens' Council, was charged with the crime. Two all-white juries failed to convict him, but thirty years later, in 1994, new evidence allowed prosecutors to reopen the case, and this time the jury found him guilty of murder. He died in prison in 2001.

The summer following Evers' murder, in 1964, three civil rights workers were murdered in Neshoba County, Mississippi, and John Salter was beaten, arrested, and seriously injured in a car "accident" of suspicious nature. All these crimes occurred during the administration of the bland, grandfatherly Ross Barnett.

That summer of 1963 I became aware for the first time of two new voices in the civil rights movement. Up in Central Harlem, a man named Malcolm X was delivering angry speeches, and down in Atlanta, Martin Luther King Jr. had begun organizing a civil rights march on Washington, DC.

In August, after my job in East Harlem had ended, Reverend Collins took several busloads of his parishioners to the March on Washington. I was driving back to Texas, and somewhere between Joplin, Missouri, and Tulsa, Oklahoma, heard Dr. King's famous "I Have a Dream" speech on the radio. It was an inspiration to me and to millions of others of my generation.

BROOKLYN 1965

Two years later, I spent the summer working as a student volunteer for the Brooklyn Protestant Parish, this time serving in a Methodist church in Bedford-Stuyvesant. Parts of that neighborhood had burned during rioting in the summer of 1964, but we saw none of that kind of violence while I was there.

I worked with a young pastor named Lou Pojman (pronounced "Poy-man") who had grown up in Chicago and who spoke with a heavy regional accent. Lou and his pretty redheaded wife lived in a red-brick manse beside a red-brick church, in a neighborhood that had been abandoned by whites and reoccupied by immigrants from the West Indies, most of them from the Bahamas.

Lou put me in charge of the high school youth group, and I began the summer thinking that I would be working with "slum kids." That notion soon evaporated. One evening we went out for pizza. Walking back to the church, two of the boys got into a discussion about Hegel, the German philosopher.

I had tried to read Hegel at the University of Texas, in the disciplined environment of a philosophy class, and had found his writing as opaque as cement. My "slum kids" had checked books out of the public library and were reading Hegel on their own. I was humbled.

They were such a lively group, I asked if they would be interested in putting on a play. I would write and direct, they would make costumes and act, and we would give a performance in the church sanctuary. They were excited and we went to work. I wrote the script and ran off copies on the church's mimeograph machine. We did rehearsals and gave our performance on a Sunday evening. Lou Pojman liked it so much, he suggested that we perform it in other churches, which we did, riding to our gigs on the subway.

I enjoyed the time I spent in New York and admired the toughness, resilience, and intelligence of New Yorkers. On the surface, they often came across as hard and cynical, but they were always kind to me, and I never felt threatened or afraid. The nearest I came to any kind of violence occurred when a white barber snarled at me because I didn't give him a tip.

New Yorkers had peculiar ideas about tipping. I, a Texas lad, wondered . . . why would anyone tip a barber? How about doctors or nurses, bus drivers, subway conductors, snow-cone peddlers . . . where did it end? It struck me as a form of extortion or bribery, and it almost got me into fights with barbers, bartenders, waiters, and taxi drivers. It was never enough for them.

Beyond that, I loved New York and figured that I would end up living there.

CHAPTER 8

AUSTIN AND ST. JOHNS

Like many in our generation, Kris and I were deeply affected by the murder of Martin Luther King Jr. Just at the moment when it appeared that America had finally decided to face the sin of slavery, a mindless little nobody with a rifle killed the one man in the US who had the moral stature to lead us to a better place.

We wanted to do something to serve our country, but what? Sitting in a college classroom seemed a cowardly thing to do. We considered volunteering for the Peace Corps and even applied for an appointment to Afghanistan but decided instead to move back to Austin and work in the area of race relations.

From Boston, we drove to Chicago to spend a few days with my old friend, Naboth Mbawa. We had worked together in East Harlem during the summer of 1963 and had stayed in touch. He had spent Christmas 1965 with me and my parents in Perryton.

In Chicago, Naboth was attending medical school and had married Evelyn, a nursing student from Rhodesia. They planned to finish their schooling and move back home, practice medicine, and help build the independent nation of Zimbabwe.

We stayed in their apartment in downtown Chicago and parked our car and trailer in a shady spot near MacArthur Park, never suspecting that bandits targeted that space for Southern white boys who came to town pulling U-Haul trailers. After the thieves had finished shopping, most of our wedding gifts and my banjo had vanished. With a much lighter load, we drove on to Austin.

During my undergraduate years at UT, I had done some volunteer work in a small Black community called St. Johns in Northeast Austin and had lived there for a year with two other UT students. I had made several friends in the community and felt that it might be a good place to establish a race relations ministry. I called it Ministry Among Neighbors.

Kris and I rented a house in the St. Johns community, and I found twelve suburban churches, both Protestant and Catholic, that were willing to pay me a small salary. I served those congregations as a race relations consultant, trying to bridge the gap between St. Johns and the affluent, mostly white suburbs that were growing around it. All of a sudden, white people and Black people were living in close proximity, sharing the same streets, schools, and shopping areas, and neither side had been prepared for it.

From my experience as a white man living in an all-Black community, I tried to explain the peculiar ways of white people to our Black neighbors, and to explain the peculiar ways of Black people to the white church members. Most of my church work occurred at night, which gave me the opportunity to write during the day.

There were striking differences between the St. Johns community and the suburban neighborhoods that were springing up around it. The suburbs had fenced yards, well-kept lawns, winding paved streets, and expensive ranch-style homes. St. Johns was a quiet, sleepy little "colored town," a collection of modest-to-shabby single-level houses built along dirt streets and separated by vacant pastureland.

I would guess that the community covered one square mile and had a population of three hundred people. It had its own elementary school, two churches, and two small business establishments. Swain's Recreation Parlor had several pool tables and sold soda pop and candy, and the proprietor handed out Jehovah's Witnesses tracts to his customers. Willie Bartee ran a small grocery store during the week and pastored a church on Sunday.

Standing outside our house, we could hear the hum and roar of traffic on Interstate 35, a mile to the west, but St. Johns was a piece of Americana that had hardly changed in the last fifty years. Many of the residents kept chickens, goats, and even a milk cow, and raised big gardens. I had seen communities like it in East Texas, Louisiana, and Mississippi, tucked away behind trees.

Several times, I asked my friends about the history of the community: why was it there, where did people come from, when was it first settled? No one knew or seemed to have much interest in history, so I had to come up with my own speculations. I guessed that the community originated in the 1920s or 1930s and that it functioned as a service population for the city of Austin, providing affordable housing for people who worked as maids, gardeners, laborers, and employees of hotels, restaurants, and hospitals.

Our neighbors were puzzled that a young white couple had moved into their community and some never accepted that I was doing church work. Decades of segregation and separation had made them suspicious of any white people who came into St. Johns. Some residents seemed sure that, once I settled in, I would reveal my true intentions—cultivating Black women or bootlegging liquor. Others believed I was an insurance salesman or an undercover policeman.

One teenage boy who lived down the street was convinced that I worked for the CIA. I wondered what he thought the CIA might hope to accomplish in a sleepy rural community in Central Texas.

FOOTBALL

Early on, I figured out that my best way of getting acquainted with the young men in the area was to participate in games of football. Every Saturday and Sunday afternoon in the fall, they assembled on the playground behind the school, chose sides, and played touch football. It was not unusual for us to have two teams of eleven players, with substitutes standing on the sidelines, and the players ranged from skinny junior high school students to grown men in their late twenties.

Kids from St. Johns provided a steady stream of athletes to Reagan High School (now Northeast Early College High School), and it was a source of pride that their little community had sent several men into professional football and baseball. They accepted as fact that they could run faster, throw farther, and jump higher than anyone with white skin.

The males of this community regarded sports as *their* domain, and my presence on the playing field produced a lot of good-natured teasing. They couldn't hold back their amusement that a white guy had dared to enter their game. They didn't push their ribbing to the point of making me feel unwelcome, but it was clear that I had something to prove.

I did this by keeping my mouth shut and taking a position in the offensive line, protecting our quarterback from the rush of the defensive linemen. Most of my teammates preferred the glory positions (quarterback, running back, and wide receiver), and left the blocking positions to the boys who were young, slow, and not well coordinated.

I had played in the offensive line on my high school football team and had learned how to hold my own against bigger men: fire off the ball and deliver a stinging blow with the shoulder and forearm, and do it over and over until the last play of the game. Never slow down and never let up. A bigger man will try to crush your resolve in the early part of the game, but if you keep hitting him and show no signs of fear or fatigue, at some point he will begin to fade.

That was the strategy I used in the touch football games. I picked out the biggest man on the opposing team (the one the younger boys tried to avoid), lined up across from him, and hit him as hard as I could on every play. When we collided, it made a loud pop. The other players noticed and were impressed. I won their respect.

After I had played a few games in St. Johns, my friends told me about some of the men I had blocked. One had killed a man with a knife. Another was AWOL from the Marine Corps and eventually ended up in prison. Another was a notorious "winehead" who had squandered an opportunity to play professional baseball.

Another, named Roydell, must have been about 6′2″ and weighed around 230 pounds, and we butted heads in several games. After one of the games, we were joking around and I noticed that he had several days' growth of beard on his broad face. I said, "What's the deal, don't you own a razor?" He grinned and said, "Oh yeah, I got one." He reached into his pocket and pulled out a straight razor with a four-inch blade.

The only man I couldn't block in touch football was a fellow named Lee Isaacs, a quiet, easygoing man with a handsome ebony face and a pleasant smile. Everyone called him Lee-Lee. He wasn't a big man, about my size, but tightly muscled like a tiger, and incredibly quick.

In touch football games, he figured out that he couldn't run over me or beat me head on, so he developed the tactic of looping outside, around the end. The first time he pulled this trick, I thought, "He can't do that again. Nobody is that fast." But he did, over and over. He was so quick, even when I knew what he was going to do, I couldn't block him.

He still had his front teeth, including one of glittering gold, but had lost several of the back ones. He worked at odd jobs and kept a goat tethered near his house. He called the goat Lawn Mower, which he pronounced "Lawn Moe."

One day I gave Lee a ride to a motel where he hoped to get a job. They gave him a form to fill out, and I discovered that he was illiterate. He was ashamed that I discovered this inability. He had hidden it very well.

A STORYTELLER

After Kris and I had been living in the community for several months, we established a friendship with a young couple, Bonnie and Henry Gordon, that lived about a block from us on Bethune Avenue. They had married right out of high school and had a baby boy, and we found that we had a lot in common.

They liked us and we liked them, and we often got together for supper at one house or the other. Like us, they had little money to spend and enjoyed the simple pleasures of getting together with friends. Sometimes, after supper, we played dominoes. At other times they put on a record and danced to James Brown or the Temptations.

Bonnie and Henry danced as naturally as they breathed and walked. For me, dancing was as foreign as ice skating, owing in part to the fact that I had grown up in a church that didn't approve of it. There were also genetic problems. My Swedish and Scots-Irish chromosomes had a blank in the slot reserved for dancing.

Henry tried to teach me a few moves on the dance floor and took devilish delight in mocking my efforts. "Naw, man, you move like Frankenstein! You . . . you look like you been dead for two weeks. Loosen up your arms and move your booty around." I tried, but my booty didn't move very well.

Some evenings we just sat around and talked. Bonnie and Henry were curious about white people, and Kris and I were just as eager to hear about their families and experiences. The high point of these encounters came when Henry found his groove and began telling stories.

There were other gifted storytellers in St. Johns, but Henry was the best, an exquisitely talented practitioner of the spoken word. He didn't just *talk* a story. He did voices for his characters, acted out their parts, and imitated their mannerisms and facial expressions. His tales kept us laughing for hours at a time.

At some point, I awoke to the difference between Henry's stories and those that I was writing during the day. My written stories reflected the instruction I had received in university classes. They were humorless, dark, depressing, and boring. That was the way literature had been presented to us in college. "Depressing" seemed to be one of the defining characteristics of serious literature, successful plays, and "important" movies.

It sounds laughable, but young writers of my generation believed that intelligent people should be depressed about something—the Vietnam War, social problems, poverty, nuclear weapons, or whatever. If you weren't depressed, you weren't a true intellectual. You hadn't found the courage to face the Awful Truth: that we live in a godless universe and are trudging through a meaningless existence. What's to laugh about?

During my six years of living in cities and attending universities, I encountered art forms that expressed this bleak worldview, yet a tiny voice inside my soul cried out for something else. I recognized it in Henry's stories: simple, organic, innocent humor.

In my writing time, I began trying to imitate his storytelling techniques. My early efforts weren't very successful (I had to unlearn a lot of bad habits), but this new approach started me on a path that, years later, led to Hank the Cowdog. The Hank stories reflect the oral tradition of my mother's ranching heritage, but it was Henry Gordon who made me aware of it.

I learned more about storytelling from him than from any other human, book, or institution. I owe him a huge debt of gratitude.

OPERATION BROTHERHOOD

As part of my interracial ministry, I started a group for high school boys, Operation Brotherhood, and asked Henry if he would work with me as a counselor. He agreed and became a vital part of its success.

Our objective was to recruit five Black kids from St. Johns and five white boys from the churches I was serving, put them together in a group, and give them a chance to get acquainted. Even though they attended the same high school, they rarely crossed the racial divide that persisted in spite of integration. Blacks stayed in their cliques and the whites stayed in theirs.

At this time in American history, Blacks and whites knew very little about each other. Young white liberals like me had met a few Black students in college and had read some books on the subject of race relations, and we were inclined to think that Blacks and whites were about the same, only with different skin pigment and hair texture. That served as the conventional wisdom on college campuses, where cultural differences were masked by the common experience of belonging to the same academic institution.

But living inside a community of working-class Black people, and observing them up close every day, caused me to question these facile assertions. Truth compelled me to admit that my friends and neighbors in St. Johns were quite different from anyone in my family and hometown. We were so different, we might have come from different countries. In fact, we did. They came from an African heritage, and I was a Northern European.

We had major cultural and social differences that weren't imaginary. Racial integration didn't resolve the problems that were bound to arise when the two groups were thrown together. The question was, what did we do about it?

The boys from St. Johns had grown up poor and had a tough, self-reliant quality that I admired. The white kids, most from upper middle-class homes with college-educated parents, seemed soft and pampered by comparison. I felt that each group could benefit from exposure to the other, as I had benefited from my friendship with Henry.

Henry and I set the pattern for Operation Brotherhood: a Black man and a white man who had been raised under very different circumstances, who had racial and cultural differences, but who had found enough common ground to become friends. We established a model of trust and respect and hoped the boys would follow it.

Our group met every Sunday afternoon in a home of one of the boys, one week in St. Johns, the next week in a white neighborhood, and we made it clear that the host was responsible for making it a pleasant experience for everyone in the group—pleasant and *safe*. America and the South had come a long way since the Long Hot Summers of 1963–64, but safety was a subject we had to address.

One ugly incident would have sunk our group. That never happened and I'm sure that part of the reason was that, from the beginning, we brought everyone's uneasiness out into the open. We worked hard to establish trust.

In addition to our weekly meetings, we planned projects and field trips. Henry and I took the boys on a two-day canoeing and camping excursion on Lake Travis. Bill Culp, a man who attended one of my church discussion groups, worked as a scientist and had connections at NASA. He suggested that we take our Operation Brotherhood lads on a tour of NASA's facility in Friendswood, outside of Houston. Bill set it up for us and even arranged for us to meet Buzz Aldrin, one of the astronauts who had walked on the moon.

REFLECTIONS ON ST. JOHNS

Kris and I found much to love and admire about our friends in the St. Johns community, their warmth, spontaneity, resilience, and expressiveness. I often found myself comparing these qualities to my own white middle-class Protestant upbringing and wishing that I were more expressive of my emotions.

But we also got a look at a darker side of the culture. People who find it easy to express feelings of joy and happiness tend to be just as unrestrained in their anger. In some ways, our time in St. Johns was like living in the Wild West. People in the community rarely called the police and tended to settle their own disputes, and sometimes these took a violent turn.

One night, while Kris and I were playing chess, two winos got into a gunfight in the street in front of our house. We turned out the lights and hit the floor. Fortunately, both men were so drunk, they missed each other, but they did send a stray bullet through the window of a sweet elderly lady who lived next door to us.

One of our neighbors was a crippled man who couldn't talk. I asked Henry if he'd had a stroke. "No, his old lady caught him messing around with another woman and wrapped an iron skillet around his head."

A woman who lived across the street from us got tired of her husband's drinking. One night when he was drunk, she tied him, spread-eagled, to the bedposts and beat him with an electrical cord until he wet himself. He was a big hulk of a man, she a timid wisp of a woman.

One Sunday afternoon Henry and I joined some other men who were playing basketball at the St. Johns school. Henry got into an argument with a man named Squeaky that escalated into hard words, shouts, and pushing. Henry told Squeaky to go get his gun and meet him in a certain place.

Since I had ridden to the game in Henry's car, this put me in an awkward position, and I told him that I really didn't want to attend a shootout. He laughed and said, "He won't show up." We drove to the spot and waited. Much to my relief, Henry turned out to be right. Squeaky didn't show up with his gun.

PART 3

BACK TO THE PRAIRIE

CHAPTER 9

JOE AND ANNA BETH

"Leave them alone and they will come home / Bringing their tails behind them."

—"Little Bo-Peep," Mother Goose

When I left Harvard Divinity School, I remained, technically, a student on a year's leave of absence. I renewed my leave of absence for the 1969–70 school year and continued my work with Ministry Among Neighbors. I wasn't sure that I wanted to go back to HDS and finish the three hours of course work that would complete my Master of Theological Studies degree, but I didn't know what else to do.

I wanted to expand my interest in writing, but how? I decided to look into the possibility of going to graduate school at UT. I set up an appointment with the graduate advisor in the Department of English and met with him in his book-lined office. I told him that I wanted to be a writer: I had written plays, essays, articles, and book reviews, and had started a novel.

He looked at me for a long moment. "If you want to be a writer, why would you come *here*?"

The question caught me by surprise, and I stammered, "Well, you deal with literature . . . authors, novels, writing."

His gaze swept the ceiling. "Mr. Erickson, the people at this place talk about other peoples' books. We don't write. We grade papers. We teach. If you want to write, just do it and don't waste your time in graduate school."

I was stunned. I couldn't believe he'd said that! I fumed about it for days but came to the conclusion that I had been in the company of a wise man. He must have sensed I would have made a lousy graduate student and would never have been happy in that environment.

Over the years, I encountered college instructors who, after a few drinks, expressed regrets that they went into teaching and never got back to that novel they started in college. They married, and children came, then house payments, car repairs, braces for the kids. College teaching gave them a steady income and a place to hang their hat—and a perfect excuse not to write. I wouldn't have been satisfied with that.

MY PARENTS

When Kris and I were students at UT, Austin was a sleepy little provincial capital with a population of 180,000. By the spring of 1970, it had entered into a period of explosive growth and was changing into a bustling metropolis with chronic traffic snarls and sprawling suburbs.

As I watched paving crews bury huge swaths of fertile ground beneath asphalt, I could almost hear the grass crying out. I didn't like the city that Austin was becoming.

I felt that my work with Ministry Among Neighbors had served its purpose and it was time for us to move on down the road. We left the St. Johns community with many pleasant memories and hopes that our two years of interracial ministry had done some good. Kris and I took none of the heavy risks that were commonplace to Medgar Evers, John Salter Jr. (who later changed his name to John Hunter Gray to honor his Native American heritage), Martin Luther King Jr., and many others, but we did make an effort. We thought it was something worth doing.

We weren't sure where we were going when we left Austin, but we thought it might be fun to spend some time in Vancouver, British Columbia. Perhaps we'd seen some travel brochures. We left busy Austin, pulling a two-wheel trailer loaded with our worldly possessions, and drove 550 miles north to Perryton, where we planned to spend a few days washing clothes and visiting my parents.

But we lingered.

In college, I had learned to view my parents as "Babbitts," a name invented by Sinclair Lewis and put into service by the students of my generation. It allowed us to dismiss the accomplishments of our parents with a single word, identifying them as members of a narrow-minded, provincial bourgeoisie who practiced an unenlightened form of Christianity, grubbed for money in small businesses, and filled their time with the hollow rituals of ticky-tacky little towns.

But while staying in my parents' home and sharing their companionship, I began to realize that, during my eight years away from home, I had forgotten who they were. They weren't Babbitts. They were Joe and Anna Beth: fine, unselfish, civilized human beings, and I liked them.

Michael Medved was a student at Yale at the same time I was at Harvard Divinity School. Although our backgrounds were quite different (he grew up in California, the son and grandson of Jewish immigrants from Russia), we both came through the storm of the sixties with a renewed respect for our parents and for the country that had bestowed so many blessings on them (Medved 2004, 15–16).

My parents were born more than a thousand miles apart: Anna Beth Curry in Seminole, Texas, and Joseph Wiley Erickson in Independence, Missouri. She was the daughter and granddaughter of West Texas ranchers, he the son of an independent grocer who came to America from Sweden at the age of 12. The odds against my parents ever finding each other must have been astronomical.

During the Depression, Joe got tired of working in the family grocery store with his three brothers and decided to have a go at college. He told me very little about his academic experience, only that he learned some accounting skills, drank a lot of whiskey, and played enough bridge to flunk out.

I once asked if he regretted not getting a college degree and he said no. He didn't need a diploma on the wall to prove that he was intelligent. He never doubted it.

Jobs were scarce in Missouri, but a cousin living in Midland, Texas, wrote that the oil business was booming in the Permian Basin. Joe caught a train and arrived in West Texas at sunset. The vastness of the mesquite prairie might have unsettled a young man from the leafy Midwest, but he loved the broad open spaces and the big sky.

In Midland he went to work as a landman, researching land titles in small-town courthouses all over the Permian Basin. He met Anna Beth, the oldest of Buck and Mabel Curry's five daughters, in the Seminole county clerk's office.

I've wondered about Anna Beth's first impressions of Joe Erickson. He would have stood out in a crowd of men in

Seminole, clearly not a cowboy or an oil field worker. He was tall (6′1″) and thin, had clear blue eyes and wavy brown hair, and wore rimless glasses and no doubt a white shirt and a tie. At a glance, she would have detected intelligence and honesty in his gaze and known that he was a man of substance.

And his impression of her? Photographs of Anna Beth at that time reveal a woman of stunning beauty with dark hair and eyes that might have suggested a link to Italy, Greece, or Spain, but traced back to a Cherokee grandmother on her father's side, a woman about whom we know nothing.

Once they began talking, she would have learned that Joe cared nothing about horses, cattle, rodeo, or sports. He loved classical music, played the piano, and was a good bridge player. They would have discovered that they both came from Christian homes, were readers, had good senses of humor, and spoke grammatical English. I doubt that either of my parents would have married someone who was careless with language.

They didn't tell me much about their courtship. Their generation wasn't inclined to talk about matters of the heart, and I was too self-preoccupied to ask. Seminole was a two-hour drive on gravel roads from Midland and yet, somehow, they dated. Joe was a graceful dancer, and they went dancing. He got along well with Anna Beth's family. Grandmother Curry was especially fond of him, and that was no small accomplishment as she was a stern judge of people.

They decided to hold their wedding ceremony in the Curry backyard, half a mile north of the town square, instead of in a church, and I don't recall ever hearing why. There might have been some fuss over which church. Joe had grown up Presbyterian, Anna Beth a Southern Baptist. The backyard might have been a compromise, but in the long run, Baptists won. That's the church I was raised in.

They made their home in Midland, and it was there that Charles, Ellen, and I were born. During the war, when Joe served in the Pacific, we moved to Seminole and lived in a rental house next door to Anna Beth's sister Bennett, whose husband Joe Harter was also in the Pacific serving on a destroyer, and her two boys. Grampy Buck Curry owned both houses.

I was two years old when my father returned home from the war. He was anxious to see me, the child he had heard about in letters but hardly knew. He had grown a beard and when I saw him, I screamed and ran out of the room. He was furious. We got off to a rocky start.

THE MOVE TO PERRYTON

After the war, my family returned to Midland. I have only a few memories of Midland and our house on Kentucky Street, and in 1946, when I was three, we moved to Perryton, where Joe had been offered a job as a hospital administrator using skills he had acquired in the army.

It was never clear to me why my parents decided to leave Midland, but I think it had something to do with Joe's favorite cousin, Ada. She and her husband had prospered in the oil business and belonged to Midland's wealthy elite. Their lives centered around activities at the country club, and "Aunt Ada," as we called her, insisted that my parents become a part of the club set.

She was a formidable presence, a small woman with a sharp tongue and an iron will. She told everyone what to do and usually got her way. The Joe Erickson I knew years later had a powerful instinct to resist any kind of manipulation, but he found it hard to say no to his cousin.

The result was that Joe and Anna Beth spent several years learning the basic lesson that you can't pursue a champagne life on a beer income. The country club swirl left them in debt and may have put a strain on their marriage. I would guess that my mother figured out that the only solution was to put a lot of West Texas miles between Joe and his cousin, so we moved to Perryton, the northernmost county seat in the state.

Aunt Ada was hurt and never understood why we left Midland. I suspect that my mother's intuition was right on target.

Perryton lay on the bald prairie of the Panhandle, 350 miles north of Midland. I have a few hazy memories of crossing the Canadian River bridge near Borger and following a very long, flat gravel road the last seventy miles to Perryton. The High Plains seemed infinite, rather forbidding, and cold. When I read Tolstoy and Dostoevsky, their descriptions of the Russian countryside stirred old memories of the Panhandle.

We lived several weeks in the Perryton Hotel, a three-story yellow-brick building that was the tallest structure in town, while Joe and some carpenters remodeled an old two-story house he had bought on the south edge of Perryton. When we moved into the house, each of us kids had our own room on the second floor and each room had its own open-flame gas heater. Amherst Street at that time was unpaved.

The house had no insulation (Joe took care of that a few years later) and it was cold in the winter. A strong north wind rattled the old wooden windows, and the curtains stirred in the gusts. My mother supplied us with plenty of army surplus wool blankets (she used the old cowboy word "suggan" instead of "blanket") and, to stay warm, I slept with one over my head.

I have deep-rooted memories of being inside the warm space of a wool blanket, listening to the howls and moans of the north wind. It is a habit that has persisted throughout my life. I still sleep with a blanket over my head.

In Perryton, Joe became the administrator of a family-owned hospital. He was competent, decisive, and popular with the staff, but got embroiled in a personality clash with one of the owners, a doctor whose behavior showed indications of mental health issues and who was a closeted alcoholic. He could be charming one day and a complete monster the next, and he had a talent for tormenting people who lacked the power to resist his bullying, especially the nurses. Joe hired the nurses, and it was to him they went in tears, so he had to confront the doctor. "Leave the nurses alone, or I'll resign."

The doctor smiled. "Oh, you will, huh? You have a wife and three children to support, and you just bought that old two-story house on Amherst. You can't afford to quit this job, Joe. You need me a lot more than I need you."

Joe cleaned out his desk and walked out the door. It was an act of genuine heroism, because the doctor had been right. Joe needed the job and didn't have a good fallback strategy.

He gave himself a month to do nothing but think and plan. At the end of the month, he paid a visit to the First National Bank to apply for a loan. He asked to speak with Carl Ellis, the bank president, but Mr. Ellis was not available, so he was directed to one of the vice presidents.

Joe said, "I would like to borrow five thousand dollars." The banker asked what he intended to do with it. "I want to borrow five thousand dollars. Will you loan it to me?" The banker said, "Not unless you tell me what you plan to do with it." Joe thanked him and left.

A day or so later, he set up an appointment with Mr. Ellis. "I want to borrow five thousand dollars. Will you loan it to me?" Mr. Ellis looked him over with a pair of hard banker's eyes and said, "Yes, I will."

Decades later, when Joe told me this story, I asked why

he had been so stubborn about discussing the loan. He said, "Bankers rent money. I wanted to rent some of their money, and what I planned to do with it was none of their business. All they needed to know was that I would pay it back. Mr. Ellis thought that I would, and I did."

I am a loyal customer of Mr. Ellis's bank.

Joe used the loan to set himself up in the insurance and real estate business, another brave action in a town where he had no ties with the old money and was considered an outsider. On Main Street, he competed against three other businesses that had been in the same families for two generations. He operated that business for thirty-five years.

The doctor who had started the trouble at the hospital didn't do as well. He sank deeper into alcoholism and mental illness and eventually took his own life.

As an independent businessman who kept an office on Main Street, Joe had to cultivate a public personality that allowed him to function in the world of commerce. His customers and associates in the Rotary Club and Chamber of Commerce saw him as open, honest, affable, intelligent, and witty, and indeed he was.

But he was also a very private man, skilled at controlling the access to his deepest thoughts. When I was growing up, the last of three children, he wasn't an easy man to know. He and Anna Beth had a clear division of labor. He went out every day, battled the world, and made a living. She ran the house and raised the children. His work and civic duties kept him away from home much of the time.

He also served as organist at the First Baptist Church, which demanded a great deal of his time. He had to be at his instrument for worship services on Sunday morning and evening, at Wednesday night prayer meeting, and every night of the week when we had revivals. He was often called upon to play at weddings and funerals and spent Saturday afternoons practicing the organ alone in the empty sanctuary.

He was a man who had great respect for books. We were not people of wealth, but we always had enough money to buy books to display in the living room where visitors would see them. My parents were proud of their library, but I wouldn't describe Joe as bookish or scholarly. He wasn't one to hole up with a stack of books and spend a Sunday afternoon reading. He kept a Bible close at hand and read it in short bursts.

I doubt that he read many of the classics of literature, although we had some of them in the library. It is also possible that, like me, he was a slow reader, although he never said so. I'm not sure where his love of books came from. I don't remember that his parents or brothers were bookish at all. They were more of a type that might read the morning newspaper and a few things relating to business, and little else. Our family library may have been an echo of Buck and Mabel and our Quaker kinfolks back in Estacado. In other words, Anna Beth might have been the book lover, while Joe came to it through marriage.

When he was around the house, he enjoyed listening to classical music, working on crossword puzzles, and playing the piano. He was an adult's adult and didn't particularly enjoy the company of children, his or anyone else's. He didn't play with me when I was young or share my interest in football, hunting, fishing, or camping.

The truth is, he knew very little about being a child. During the Depression, he and his three brothers worked long hours in the family grocery store. They had no time for sports or extra-curricular activities in school. They learned to work at an early age and that's all they knew.

Joe was a strict disciplinarian, and his discipline was seldom loud or angry, always swift and fair. He kept his paddle in a large walk-in closet, and when he said, "Come wiss me to zee casbah," I received swats. The line about the casbah came from the trailer of an old movie, set in Algeria. I never saw the movie, but growing up, I heard the line many times and deserved every swat I received.

We did have one tense episode when I was in the ninth or tenth grade. I was feeling my oats and had outgrown Mother's flyswatter discipline. One day I mouthed off to her. Joe heard it, came thundering into the room, escorted me into the casbah, and closed the door. He said that if I was too big to spank, we could work it out with our fists, but one way or another, I was never to treat my mother that way again.

I had gotten my growth by then and for a few hard-eyed seconds, I wondered if I could whip him. But it was a question I didn't want to answer. I humbled myself and said, "Yes, sir," and stopped tormenting my poor little mother. That was the end of it.

I didn't always like my father, but I did respect him. If you believe that a father should be a buddy to his children, he came up short, but he gave me a model of a strong, godly man who was faithful to his family and honest in his dealings with the public: kind, wise, and generous.

With such a man, the word "Babbitt" does not apply. It might have described Sinclair Lewis's father, but not mine.

CHAPTER 10

FARMHAND

Our stay at my parents' house stretched from days into weeks. One day Joe mentioned that one of his customers needed a man to help him with farm work. By odd coincidence, Joe had also spotted a nice little one-bedroom house that had come up for rent. He suggested that Kris and I might as well stick around for a while, and all at once that seemed like a good idea. I had begun to sense that my writing would benefit from the slow pace of a small town.

My parents had keen instincts about when to help and when to leave us alone, and living close to them gave us some protection against poverty. We moved into the rental house and Kris got busy making it into a home, something she has always done very well.

My six years of college had given me a pretty sound liberal arts education but little in the way of practical knowledge. Those of us who occupied the high ground of liberal arts often boasted that students in the business and engineering schools were merely "trained." We, on the other hand, were "educated." At the age of twenty-six, I was so "educated" that driving a tractor was one of the few marketable skills I possessed.

Through the summer and fall of 1970, I worked as a farmhand for Wendell Ferguson. Wendell lived and farmed up in the Oklahoma Panhandle, north of Perryton, and leased a section (640 acres) of farmland southwest of town.

That's where I worked six days a week. Wendell hired me to do his plowing and to handle the chores related to irrigation, which consisted of moving twenty-foot sections of aluminum pipe, setting the gates on the pipes, and keeping the irrigation motor in operating condition.

I'm sure Wendell wondered why a fellow with six years of college was working as a farmhand, but he said nothing about it. From his perspective, it was a good arrangement. I might have been odd but was also sober, honest, and reliable. I showed up for work every day and didn't make mistakes that destroyed expensive machinery. Plowing was something I had done in high school, and though it wasn't a complex skill, I did it well.

I spent most of my twelve-hour workdays alone, steering a Case tractor back and forth across wheat ground that had been harvested in June. It was dirty, noisy, tedious work, and I devised ways of passing the time. Sometimes I sang over the roar of the engine. I memorized passages from Shakespeare. I even tried to work on a novel.

If you were going to choose a place to write a novel, a tractor that is bouncing across a field would not rank high on the list, but I couldn't bear the thought of spending all those hours without doing something creative, so I figured out a way of writing on a moving tractor.

With two bands of rubber, I attached a small spiral notebook to my right thigh. Steering the tractor with my left hand, I was able to scribble on the dusty page. Once I had perfected the system, I began writing several hours every day.

This was *not* something I wanted Wendell to know about, and I practiced strategies to conceal my activities. Before leaving the house in the morning, I packed the notebook in the thermos compartment of my lunch pail. If I knew that Wendell was coming out to check on things, I kept the pad in the lunch pail so that he would never see it strapped to my thigh or lying in the cab of the tractor.

Wendell came around once a week to confirm that my disc plow was set properly or to send me to another patch of wheat stubble that needed plowing. We ate lunch together in his pickup, then he would leave to check on the other parts of his operation.

Wendell was a tall man, probably 6′3″, and as lean as a bull snake. His manner of dress never changed: blue jeans, a Western-style shirt, cowboy boots, and either a straw cowboy hat or a gimme cap. He had a straight, thin mouth and didn't smile much. His gaunt face and droll expression reminded me of a greyhound that had been on short rations, and it provided good cover for his dry sense of humor.

One day he came to the field and we had lunch in his pickup. He had just come from a meeting with his banker, and they had discussed the purchase of a new tractor. Wendell's equipment was showing its age and needed to be replaced, but he was worried that he couldn't afford a new machine. The prices of wheat and cattle were down and although he worked long hours, he was having a hard time making a living in agriculture.

Every farmer and rancher in the region faced the same dilemma. Agriculture was a wonderful way of life, but not always a great way to make a living.

After a long conversation, he and the banker decided that he needed the new tractor and should borrow the money to buy it. Wendell gave me a little smirk and said, "If I get in a bind, the banker can't eat me."

We laughed and opened our lunch pails to see what our wives had prepared for us. I had forgotten about my notebook—and Wendell saw it. It happened in a split second. His gaze went to the notebook, then he looked away and said nothing. Suddenly I realized that *he already knew what I'd been doing*, and had probably known it from the very beginning, but he'd never said a word about it.

Up until that moment, I had assumed that college-educated people were quite a bit smarter than anyone who carried a lunch pail. It was a conceit I had picked up in the academic world and had absorbed without question.

That little incident with Wendell gave me a new respect for small-town and country people. They were plenty smart, but you didn't always know it because, unlike college students, *they didn't tell you.* When I figured this out, I felt humiliated and embarrassed, a sneak who had been exposed. It was a lesson I needed to learn and didn't forget.

GARAGE OFFICE

In Boston and Austin, I had acquired the discipline of writing every morning for three or four hours, giving my first and best energy to writing and what was left to a job that paid the bills. Our little rental house had a detached garage, and I furnished it with a wooden table and chair, making it my writing office.

During the months I worked on the farm, I tried to establish a regular pattern of writing, but it wasn't easy. I was working six days a week, leaving the house at 6:30 in the morning and coming back home at 7:30 in the evening. I wrote when I could on the tractor and in my little office.

Over my fifty-odd years of writing, I've done my work in some humble settings—spare bedrooms, a barn, a tool shed, a bunk house—but this office in the garage might have been the humblest. It was all right in the summer but was uncomfortable in the winter months. It had a cement floor and no insulation on the walls. On cold winter mornings, I cranked up the little gas heater as high as it would go but still had to wear a coat and a pair of wool gloves. Typing with gloves wasn't easy, but I figured out how to do it.

What was I writing in my frigid, ugly little office? Novels, short stories, book reviews, plays, and essays, and most of them haven't survived. At the time, I thought they were good and maybe they were, but not good enough to attract a publisher.

My biggest problem as a writer was that I lacked any kind of solid, sustained life-experience. What had I ever *done*? I had spent eighteen of my twenty-six years as a student of one kind or another, and that was poor preparation for a writer.

Learning inside a classroom has its place (I wouldn't have read Homer, Kant, Plato, or Shakespeare on my own), but it can also create mirages of knowledge. At the time, they appear to be as palpable as trees or mountains, but they're actually tricks the mind plays on itself. The farther we progress up the educational ladder, the more confidence we invest in the mirage.

I'm inclined to think that my generation was especially vulnerable to this defect, simply because we were the first group of mass-produced college students America had ever generated. We had no model, no parents or grandparents who had done it and against whom we could measure our experiences.

When we sort through our memories of the sixties and try to explain behavior that seems a bit crazy, it might be helpful to factor this into the equation. There we were, allegedly adults, but still taking classes. Most of us had never held a job for any length of time, rocked a crying baby in the night, planned a funeral, or made a mortgage payment.

Compared to our parents and grandparents, who had endured a world war, the Depression, and two crushing droughts, we hadn't done much of anything. For an aspiring novelist, that can be a crippling weakness.

WRITING NOVELS

The two years I'd spent living in St. Johns had given me a reservoir of story material, and my best writing effort from this period was a novel that drew on those characters and situations. I got the idea for *The Adventures of Bookie Tanner* after making a detailed study of *Tom Sawyer*, one of my favorite novels. I modeled my main character on several of my Black friends in St. Johns and let him narrate the story, just as Henry Gordon might have told it.

In many ways, *Bookie Tanner* was a big step forward—a funny story, told in a strong storytelling voice, and involving nothing I had ever observed on a college campus. I was proud of that story and sent it off to dozens of publishing houses. It drew some encouraging rejection slips, but several editors pointed out that a white author, writing honestly about Black characters, might be accused of being "racially insensitive."

This was my first exposure to political correctness, at a time when the term had not yet been invented, and it made me furious. It was okay for James Baldwin, Eldridge Cleaver, and LeRoi Jones (now Amiri Baraka) to write all kinds of unflattering descriptions of white people, but somehow it was "insensitive" of me to write about Black characters I had known and events I had witnessed with my own eyes?

I assumed that I was being scolded by lily-white English major editors who grew up in lily-white upper-class suburbs, made top grades in Ivy League colleges, and had read all the Right Books, but who had never even considered doing what Kris and I had done—spent two years right in the middle of living, breathing, sweating, laughing, yelling Black people, some of whom we loved and some of whom we didn't.

But it was an argument I had no chance of winning. In *Bookie Tanner*, I was writing about a culture that didn't belong to me, at a time when people with power said it wasn't permitted. I needed to find story material in my own culture but was still years away from accomplishing that goal.

The one piece of writing that survived the Farmhand Period was a historical novel, set on the Texas frontier in 1874 but with an odd twist. It appeared to be a "Western" novel, yet the story was patterned on the *Epic of Gilgamesh* which was written on clay tablets in ancient Mesopotamia around 3000 BC. It is the oldest written story known to man, and I found it fascinating when I read it at the University of Texas.

I began scratching out thoughts and ideas for the Gilgamesh book on the tractor, and later finished a first draft of about 300 pages. It sat in a box for years, then in the early 1980s I dusted it off and did a major revision. In 1982, I sent it to Pat LoBrutto, a Westerns editor at Doubleday I had met at a writers' convention, and he liked it.

I made the revisions he suggested, he paid me a $2,500 advance, and the book came out as a Double D hardcover Western in 1983 with a new title: *The Hunter*. The Double D line of Western novels focused on the library market, so it never appeared on a bookstore shelf and soon faded into obscurity.

Doubleday didn't mention that my novel had been inspired by a story written five thousand years ago.

CHAPTER 11

THE COUNTRY CLUB

I worked on the farm through the summer and fall of 1970, plowing stubble ground, then planting wheat in September. October brought the milo harvest, and I drove a truck for Wendell while he operated the combine. When the milo harvest ended in November, there was no more work on the farm until spring.

Kris and I had settled into our life as members of a small town and had lost our desire to wander. I had established a routine of rising early every morning and writing for several hours in my little office in the garage. Kris had found a circle of friends and had started doing macramé and pottery.

We were happy with the simple, slow pace of life in Perryton, and enjoyed living close to my parents. But I had to find another way of making a living.

Once again, it was my father who heard about a position, this time at the local country club, a private corporation that offered its stockholders a touch of elegant white-tablecloth dining and a place to entertain business contacts. Not the least of its attractions was that it offered its members the opportunity to purchase beer, wine, and mixed drinks in a bar that operated in a "dry" county.

Dean McLain, the manager, was Perryton-raised and I had known him and his family all my life. His wife Marty had been my speech teacher in high school. I performed the lead role in her senior play, Noël Coward's *Blithe Spirit*, and participated in one-act play and debate.

When I interviewed for the job of assistant manager, I told Dean about my unusual situation: I wanted to set my hours so that I could write in the mornings. He said that would work out fine. I could come in at 10:30 in the morning, help with the lunch run, stay through the afternoon when the cooks and waitresses went home, and leave around five or six in the evening when the night shift came to work.

Sometimes, though, he would need to switch my hours around and I would have to work nights (parties, special events, club dances), and there might be times when he would need me as the backup bartender. (Bartenders were a restless breed. They came and went.) It happened that I had taken a bartending course in Boston, so that worked out well. I got the job.

TEXANS AND LIQUOR

In Texas, each county had the option of voting itself "wet" or "dry." This was a legacy that went back to the Prohibition laws of the twenties. When the federal government repealed the Prohibition laws, a lot of rural counties in Texas opted to remain dry. In 1970, every county north of the Canadian River was dry, meaning that, in theory, you couldn't buy a drink or bottle that contained beer, liquor, or wine.

Our county, Ochiltree, had been dry for four decades—or "moist" might be more accurate. Perryton always had a stable of bootleggers who worked in the shadows. A friend of my parents owned a drugstore in the forties and worked with a retired physician who wrote prescriptions for whiskey,

Several efforts to repeal the dry laws had failed. The debate had taken on a theological cast, with the Mennonites, Church of Christ, and five or six varieties of Baptists arguing that liquor would ruin the community, while the Presbyterians, the Catholics, and the unchurched took the position that it would improve the economy and help the city fathers bring new business to town.

The Methodists worked both sides of the street, as they often do. Some were staunch prohibitionists, while others pointed out that the moderate consumption of wine had more scriptural support than, say, brushing your teeth.

The Dries had the votes and won at the ballot box, so the Wets (not just in our county but all over the state) made a shrewd end run and pushed a bill through the legislature, allowing "private clubs" to serve drinks to their members.

The Perryton Club fell into the category of a private club, a corporation that served only its stockholder-members. Under the law, members had to provide their own spirits, and we kept each member's bottles in a set of wooden lockers, each bottle bearing the member's number.

Perryton wasn't as dry as it appeared to be; the river had merely moved underground.* During the seventies, the town

* In 2013, the county voted itself wet for the first time in eighty years. Perhaps the Dries had grown complacent, or maybe they were just overwhelmed by the influx of oil field workers who had come to town, following a boom in horizontal drilling. Overnight, our United Supermarket was transformed.

had five private clubs slaking the thirst of those who could afford the price of joining: the Elks Lodge, the Moose Lodge, the VFW, the Perryton Club, and a little joint on the north side of the railroad tracks.

At the club, when members came into the bar (we called it "the lounge") and ordered a drink, the bartender had to go to their locker and bring out their bottles. On a busy Saturday night, there might be forty or fifty bottles lined up behind the bar. It was an awkward system for the bartender, but it worked well for the cooks and waitresses, who sometimes broke the monotony of a long day by borrowing a nip or two from a member's stash. The lockers were not secured, and management never inventoried the booze.

My first day on the job, I worked as a busboy and cleaned tables. I considered the work demeaning and felt a keen sense of humiliation—I, the son of good middle-class parents, had gone off to college and was now back home, bussing dishes in front of the people I had known all my life. They wondered what the heck I was doing there and I couldn't tell them. How can you tell someone you're a writer if you haven't published anything?

Cleaning tables that day, I felt very conspicuous, and it didn't help when one of the prominent ladies in town, a member of my parents' church, commented to the other ladies at her table, "My, my. We must have the best-educated busboy in Texas!" She didn't say that with any malice and was just expressing aloud what everyone else was thinking, but it did nothing to make me think that I was going to enjoy working at the club.

Although I had been hired as "assistant manager," the title meant nothing. I was just a flunky who did whatever had to be done. I took food orders in the lounge, served as backup

(note, cont.) Potato chips and dog food moved aside, making way for a store-long aisle loaded with beer and wine.

bartender, greeted customers during the lunch run, and typed monthly statements in the afternoons. Beyond that, I tried to stay out of the wars that were always breaking out between the waitresses and the cooks, and the waitresses and the bartender. I swallowed my pride and tried to make the best of it.

WRITING ON THE SLY

I didn't enjoy the job, but it served the purpose of giving me four hours of writing time in the mornings. That was my real life, my secret life. I had a strong sense of mission and threw myself into the task of learning the craft of writing. I worked on novels that never got published, wrote query letters and essays and book reviews, and kept careful notes in my journals.

I also did a good deal of reading in the early morning hours, especially books by Texas authors. (I give a detailed account of this part of my apprenticeship in later chapters.) The two Texas authors who interested me most were J. Evetts Haley and John Graves. Both were alive at that time, Mr. Haley living in Canyon and Mr. Graves near Glen Rose, and I eventually tracked them down and spent time with them.

The quality they had in common, and the one that interested me most, was that both had succeeded as "regional" writers. They had chosen to write about their own home country, and they had done it well.

It was from them that I acquired the idea of writing *Through Time and the Valley*, a book of history and folklore about the Canadian River Valley, a wild, fascinating country thirty miles south of Perryton. In 1978, it became my first published book, but I began working on it in 1970. I started my research by reading everything I could find on local history (there wasn't much), then used my days off to drive down to the river and interview ranchers and old-timers.

I did some of my reading at the club, in the afternoons when the other employees had left, and even interviewed a few customers who had knowledge of the Canadian River and its history—Ben McIntyre, H. C. Brillhart, and Bill Bartlett. Most of these interviews occurred in the bar on slow nights. Later, I typed up detailed notes while the dates and names were still fresh in my memory.

I also used my time at the club to write character sketches, like an artist drawing faces, hands, costumes, potted plants, and lamps, studies in description and detail. Writing dialogue had always been easy for me, but descriptive writing had not, so I concentrated on my area of weakness, recording details.

My usual method was to observe a subject in the lounge or dining room, jotting down brief notes on a cocktail napkin. I never carried a pocket notebook. That would have been too obvious, and the notebook might have fallen into the wrong hands.

In the afternoon, when the other employees left the club, I went to the office and typed up more complete notes, using an IBM Selectric typewriter. At that time, the Selectric was the Cadillac of writing devices, much better than the little Smith-Corona portable electric typewriter I had been using since high school.

I often typed my notes on the back of statement forms the club sent out at the end of every month. If someone came into the office while I was working, I rolled my character sketch out of the typewriter, inserted a new statement form, and went right on typing. I was living a double life, doing character sketches about people who might not have wanted to be sketched.

During those three years, I filled several notebooks with descriptions and bits of dialogue. They were sketches, not stories. A story is a literary form that begins, moves, and resolves, like the chords in a song. In resolving, it creates a unity. It takes skill to write a story that resolves, and quite a bit less talent to sketch descriptions and vignettes that merely start and stop.

My sketches described small-town people who happened to pass through my field of vision, club employees who needed a job and members who wanted to be seen in an upscale setting. Perryton was going through a period of prosperity (the oil business and cattle feeding were booming), and the club became the place of choice for tax-deductible entertainment.

Some of my sketches dealt with people who shouldn't have been there. They drank too much and destroyed their marriages, testing the limits of small-town morality. Most of those people came from sturdy middle-class stock, farmers and business owners who had learned to cope with hard times but had no preparation for leisure and prosperity.

None of that material ever found its way into a novel or short story, and it never will, because the truth is, most of us are not at our best in environments of leisure. The Prohibitionists had a valid argument. Whiskey makes us loud, vulgar, aggressive, demanding, careless, overbearing, morose, petty, and irrational.

The things a bartender observes in a saloon make good gossip and bad stories. Even so, fifty-odd years after I scribbled my notes on napkins and scraps of paper, some of the sketches might be interesting enough to share, just as I recorded them in my notes.

CHAPTER 12

CHARACTER SKETCHES

COUNTRY CLUB COWBOYS

One night last week, I was occupying my roost behind the bar, wedged in between the beer cooler and a cabinet, under a spot of light. It is to this corner that I retreat to read when I'm not mixing drinks. I was well into a second reading of Larry McMurtry's book of essays, *In a Narrow Grave.* I had been reading about "the passing of the god," as McMurtry dubs the death of the old cowboy ways in Texas.

At eleven o'clock, in walked a dozen or so members of the club who had been rehearsing a Western melodrama in another part of the building. Among them were two lawyers, a banker, and three or four Main Street businessmen. They were all decked out in Western attire, right down to scroungy hats and genuine six-shooters. Their wives were dressed as madams and dance hall girls and seemed to be enjoying their roles.

The men practiced fast-draws on one another and stared into the bores of real pistols. One fellow had brought a bugle and blew "Taps" and "Reveille," rising above the noise from the jukebox and the drone of elevator music from the speakers overhead.

The Jackson 5 came on the jukebox, and the cowboys grabbed their ladies and began to dance, while I hunched over my book and tried to concentrate on the passing of the cowboy mythology and its replacement with decadent country club society.

I managed to shut out the noise of the bugle, the Jackson 5, and even the giggles of the dance hall girls, but when one of the cowboys fired off a .45 blank, I gave up. My powers of concentration had been shattered.

MRS. WELLS

Mrs. Wells comes into the bar while her husband is with a group of men, rolling dice in the game room. She is short and dressed stylishly in a pantsuit. Her black hair stands up in a bubble shape, her green eyes are heavily lined with eye pencil. Although she is small, her voice is quite deep, due perhaps to her steady consumption of cigarettes.

She cultivates the image of being not very smart, but she has a kind of scheming intelligence. At her table in the lounge, she says to a lady friend, "My husband told me he was going to cut off my charge accounts. I said, 'Honey, if you do that, you'd better have the best lawyer between here and Georgia.'"

The other woman says she hates to write checks. Mrs. Wells brightens. "There's nothing I like better."

Her husband owns a business in the oil field and is perpetually in and out of financial trouble. No one can be sure whether they are wealthy or broke. Mrs. Wells enjoys playing the rich woman and delights in sending her food back to the kitchen.

One day at lunch, she walked into the dining room with a friend. Five tables were available, set with a cloth, silverware, and water glasses, but she wanted a table in the corner, which had not been cleaned yet.

Several employees scrambled to clear the dishes, replace the soiled tablecloth with a fresh one, and set up clean silverware, napkins, cups, water glasses, and butter dishes.

Mrs. Wells seated herself and fired up a cigarette. Out came a little spear of smoke. She turned an innocent expression toward the waitress. "You look so busy! I just love to be waited on. It makes me feel so elegant."

MRS. FARNSWORTH

She is short and thin, has long brownish-red hair which, when she wears it up, gives her a regal appearance. Sometimes she wears it pulled back in a ponytail. One suspects she does this when she doesn't want to wash it. Still other times, she lets it hang to her shoulders and looks like a crone.

She has a crisp pointed nose, a small mouth, and nice olive skin. The eyes dominate. They draw one's gaze. One moment, they appear too narrow, too dark, too far apart. They seem cunning and hard. They flick when they move. They have a way of looking through people.

At other times, they are the finest expression of a beautiful woman. They dance and sparkle when she is happy, holding a childish innocence—the charm of little girls and chipmunks.

But there are days when the sparkle is gone, when dark crescents below the eyes give them a sunken, brooding, hard look. On these days, Mrs. Farnsworth's little mouth sets naturally into a thin straight line, as though it would require great effort to raise the lips into a smile.

She can look like a queen. She can also look cheap. She often wears very short skirts in public, which she shouldn't do. It's immodest for a married woman, and she has skinny legs that look better when they're covered. She often tells bawdy jokes, is fond of juicy gossip, and has a bad habit of putting her arms around married men, even crawling into their laps.

I have a feeling that she does this to provoke her husband. One night they were in the bar with another couple. Mrs. Farnsworth sat next to the other man, and they spent the evening whispering and laughing. At some point, Mr. Farnsworth got up and left the club. An hour later, someone mentioned it to his wife. She hadn't even missed him.

LARRY THE BARTENDER

He looks fifty but acts twenty; his age is probably forty. He has a large head, greasy hair, and a little ribbon of beard that runs from ear to ear under his chin. His eyes have a reptilian quality: green glowing stones, peering out of slits of flesh. They remain the same whether he is laughing at a joke, staring at a woman's legs, or telling a customer he's had too much to drink. The pupils are dark and cold.

He laughs easily, often, and loud, and his laughter can be heard all over the club. It is not hard to identify because it usually ends in a spasm of coughing.

He is a competent bartender with years of experience. He pours the ingredients of a drink "by feel," never measuring. He makes his drinks stiff. "I can make any kind of drink except a weak one." He can get by with this in a private club, because the house doesn't own the liquor. The customers buy the bottles and most of them don't object to stiff drinks.

He seems to amuse some of the women customers. He jokes with them and flatters them with his roving eyes. To a divorcée, he says, "Wow, you look like you just walked out of *Vogue* magazine!" To a new waitress: "I'd say you get better looking every day, only you can't improve on perfection."

These same women, if they met him anywhere else, wouldn't give him a second look, but here it's part of a naughty little game.

He makes a special drink for the ladies, "Larry's Love-in." It's a pink, sweet punch, spiked with rum and served with ice in a big brandy glass. After squeezing the juice of half a lime over the top, he turns the lime inside out, floats it on the top of the drink, fills it with high octane brandy, lights it with a match, and serves it, flaming, to the lady. It's a big hit.

Larry chews Certs breath mints all the time, when he's not smoking. He drives a red and white Chevy convertible. He is a compulsive TV watcher. Since he works nights, he sees mostly daytime shows, soap operas, Westerns, and quiz shows.

When he comes to the club around four in the afternoon, the first thing he does is turn on the TV. Then he goes to the kitchen, takes a dessert out of the walk-in cooler (against club rules), comes back, flops down in a chair, and watches *Big Valley*. He never watches football or basketball. He has no interest in sports except wrestling (he pronounces it "rassling"). Sometimes he comes to work early to watch rassling.

Here is a scene I observed in the lounge, around five in the afternoon. The phone rings and Larry answers. It's a call for Mr. Spears, a cattle buyer who has been at the club for several hours, drinking dry martinis—too many. Mr. Spears takes the call in the lounge, close to where Larry is counting out quarters to put into the jukebox.

The cattle buyer talks for a while, hangs up, and turns to Larry. "That was my brother. He rolled his car, and his three-year-old daughter was killed in the wreck."

Larry looks up. “Huh. That’s really tough. Three years old. Huh.”

“I guess I’d better make some calls.”

“Sure, use the phone.”

Mr. Spears dials the operator, gives a credit card number, and puts in a long-distance call. Larry walks over to the jukebox, feeds it four quarters, and punches in a dozen of his favorite songs.

While Mr. Spears talks on the phone about the death of a little girl, the jukebox blares “Thank God and Greyhound (You’re Gone).” I’m the only one in the place who notices the hideous irony.

Larry is something of an oaf, but he has better moments. He once came out to the club in the early afternoon to attend a little birthday party for one of the waitresses, something I would never do. He also takes care of the members who drink too much—the ones who have a history of drinking too much. He keeps his eye on them, tells them when they’ve had enough, and sometimes drives them home.

The other day he revealed a sense of humor and told a story about a man who owned a bar in Amarillo. He rigged up a speaker in the commode tank in the ladies’ bathroom. When a woman went inside, he gave her time to get situated, then activated a taped message: “Excuse me, honey, but could you wait a minute and let me get out of here?”

He said the woman flew out of the bathroom, pale and screaming. Larry enjoyed telling that story, but it made him laugh so hard, he went into a fit of coughing that irritated his hernia.

Larry was fired for having an affair with a club member’s wife. He got caught in the naughty little game.

OLD BILL, THE COOK

Bill is the assistant cook (or "chef," since this is a high-class joint), working under Alvin, the head chef. Bill is tall (about 6′3″) and skinny and has the face of a buzzard: slack-jawed and toothless, long hooked nose, skinny neck, and squinty eyes.

He walks in a stiff gait as though he has a kink in his back. He rarely has much to say and when he does, he says it in a gruff voice. He drives a gigantic 1959 Cadillac and wears his high-top cook's hat even when he's off duty.

Here's a snapshot of Bill: His pants bag in the seat. His cheap shoes are splattered with spots of white paint. The skin hangs in loose ripples around his elbows. He wears a dish towel, folded into a triangle, as a neckerchief, with a piece of beef bone serving as the neckerchief slide. He carries a dishtowel stuffed into his hip pocket and uses it to wipe his hands and blow his nose. He eats Tums all the time and you rarely see him without his cook's hat.

Bill is an enthusiastic fisherman. In the back seat of his Cadillac is a minnow bucket, in the trunk, rods and reels and rubber boots. He uses waterdogs as bait and says catfish like them.

A few years back, he bought a lakeside lot for $500 and planned to retire there, close to the fish. After he had signed the papers on the property, he learned that the lake was mossed over and worthless to a fisherman. Nevertheless, he carries a card in his wallet that identifies him as the owner of lakeside property.

When Bill makes a sandwich for himself in the kitchen, he always cuts the crusts off the bread. "Gets in my teeth," he says, showing a toothless grin. He says he used to carry his false teeth in his hip pocket until one day he sat down and they bit him. Now he carries them in his shirt pocket. (I've never seen him wearing his teeth.)

Bill owns a parrot. "That bird is so smart, he ought to be going to work in the morning and I ought to be sitting in his cage." The bird can say eighty-two words and phrases, such as "Hi Bill" and "Ride 'em cowboy." Bill feeds it dog food and fruit. The bird used to eat bananas, but no more. One day, while the bird was eating a banana, Bill told him, "Bird, one of these days, you're going to turn into a monkey."

Bill was thoughtful for a moment. "I don't know if that bird understood, but from then on, he never touched another banana." Bill wanted to teach the bird how to cuss, but his wife wouldn't allow it.

His wife, Sue, is a short, dumpy woman who must be twenty years younger than Bill. She is so shy, she hardly ever talks and always walks behind him when they come to work. She runs the dishwasher in the kitchen. They have no children but keep an expensive poodle and the parrot.

Bill pretends that he doesn't care what happens in the kitchen ("They don't pay me enough to care"), but beneath his gruff exterior, he takes pride in his work and he's a good cook. Alvin, the head chef, learned his trade in the army and tends to make everything from canned ingredients. Bill prefers to cook from scratch, and he does it well. The reason he's not head chef is that he has a problem with the bottle.

SHERRY, THE COCKTAIL WAITRESS

She is thirty-five, tall, and thin, and her hair is black-dyed. Her face reminds me of a bird. The eyes are a bit off-center, so that one comes directly at you while the other looks past you. Sometimes she wears a platinum-blonde wig fixed in a beehive cut. When she wears it, she expects a compliment. If you don't give it, she will fish for it.

She works the four-to-midnight shift in the bar. She is a

tireless, exuberant, breathless worker, and often hums while she's scrambling around the bar. She talks about how she hates Larry, the bartender. She "has friends" on the board of directors and is convinced that she can get him fired. She tells me this in deepest confidence, whispering behind her hand.

The truth is, she will do anything Larry tells her to and never complains to his face. In fact, she seems to enjoy his crude and suggestive manner. They seem well suited for each other, regardless of what she says.

I got acquainted with Sherry a few days after she was hired. She came into the office, where I was typing monthly statements. She began telling me gossip about the other employees, as though I might be interested (I wasn't). "Did you know that last week, Janie came to work *drunk* and locked herself in the bathroom for three hours?"

Then she asked if she could use the phone and dialed a number. She didn't suspect that, while she talked, I was typing a transcript of her conversation.

"Hello, Dr. Jacobs? This is Sherry. I wondered if you could call in my birth control pills to the drugstore. Uh huh. Ortho-Novum. Well, we talked about that, and I think we decided on two grains. Okay, thanks."

She hung up the phone and looked at me with her crooked eyes. "A dollar ninety! Boy, what it costs to keep from getting pregnant! But it's worth it, let me tell you."

Her life is an unending soap opera, and she wants to share it with everyone. One night her babysitter called to say that her son had developed a bad cough. She ran sobbing from the club, and for days, that's all she could talk about. (The boy is fine.)

The next crisis came when her sister developed double pneumonia and tuberculosis and was on her deathbed. Sherry missed several days of work but returned after the sister had made a miraculous recovery. Then she caught her husband playing around with another woman. This was the same man she'd been madly in love with the week before. Now she tells everyone what a louse he is, and she's talking to a lawyer.

As a sign of her new defiant mood, she has changed her brand of cigarettes from Raleigh to Virginia Slims, the brand preferred by all the local women who are angry about something.

Other recent news items from Sherry's melodrama: She bought a trailer home and had her dentures worked on. She bought a new pickup. She has a $70 pantsuit on layaway. She bought a red wig. Her father was on his deathbed for a week but recovered.

I heard another story about her, and I think it might be true. She had roaches in her house but didn't want to pay a professional exterminator to get rid of them, so she did it herself. To fumigate the place, she sprayed propane into the crawl space beneath the floor, then lit up a cigarette, forgetting that propane is highly explosive. The house went off like a bomb. Sherry escaped injury, but the blast ruined her new wig.

She enjoys whipping up trouble at the club. The bartender and I almost came to blows one night in the back room, until we figured out that Sherry had been whispering to him about me and to me about him, stirring the pot to amuse herself.

When I work in the bar, I have to spend hours with this woman, and she has countless ways of getting on my nerves. One of them is that she smokes all the time, and I have to live in her cigarette fumes.

One night, I loaded several of her Virginia Slims with match heads. In her next spare moment, she reached for the pack. She had just put a wad of gum into her mouth. When she lit up, the match heads hissed and fumed, but she didn't notice until she took a big drag and inhaled the sulfur.

She made a face and stubbed out the cigarette, muttering about how the lousy cigarette had ruined the taste of her gum. She reached into her mouth to throw away the gum, but it had stuck to her false teeth, and both gum and dentures went into the trash.

I was laughing so hard I had to leave the building. Sherry never figured out why her cigarette tasted so bad.

CHAPTER 13

BORDER TOWN

I worked at the Perryton Club until the spring of 1973, when I found a job with a local company that was involved in a large cattle-feeding operation. Again, one of the attractions of the job was that it allowed me to keep my writing schedule in the early morning.

I had worked around livestock most of my life but had no particular skills that qualified me for a job in the cattle-feeding industry. I got the position because one of the company owners (we'll call him Jake) discovered that I played chess. He loved the game and was good at it. He hired me because he wanted to have a chess opponent close at hand.

Jake owned enough stock in the company that he could do pretty much as he pleased. When the atmosphere in the office became oppressive, he would decide that he and I needed to make a trip to check on one of the firm's farming operations.

The company kept two airplanes at the local airport, a

twin-engine Beechcraft King Air that required the services of an instrument-rated pilot, and a smaller single-engine craft. Jake was licensed to fly the smaller plane, though I was never convinced that he was qualified.

He was an intelligent man but a bit scatterbrained and forgetful, and flying with him always made me nervous. He was the kind of man who might do a preflight check of the radio, compass, and navigation system but forget to gas up the plane.

One evening we were flying back to Perryton. The sun had dropped beneath the horizon and the cabin was growing dark, so Jake flipped on the dash lights. They had shorted out and he couldn't read his instruments.

He grinned and said, "I think we can make it. I've got a flashlight." But the flashlight didn't work either.

I knew that Kris would be disappointed if I ended up in a heap of burning rubble on the Perryton runway, and I conveyed this to Jake in the strongest terms I could come up with. He uttered a sigh and we landed at sunset in Pampa, sixty miles short of our destination.

When we made short trips (two hundred miles or less), we flew in the single-engine plane. Jake would take it up to ten thousand feet, level off, and engage the automatic pilot. Then, grinning, he would say, "Set 'em up."

I would pull out the small chessboard we carried in the plane and set up pieces that had magnets to hold them on the board. For the next hour, Jake paid scant attention to the airplane and concentrated on beating me in chess. He was a meticulous player. If he ever got a one-pawn advantage, I couldn't beat him because he didn't make careless mistakes. He would grind it out to the end and wouldn't allow me to concede the game.

When we arrived at our destination (a farm operation with no airstrip), Jake would circle the property, looking for the best dirt-road landing strip. Sometimes he had to dive-bomb cattle or deer to shoo them off the road.

In April, Jake announced that we were going to fly down to McAllen on the Mexican border. The company had been buying a large number of Mexican cattle and Jake aimed to "check things out." He wanted to escape from the office and knew that the cattle buyers in McAllen would show him a good time.

I would have preferred skipping this trip. In Texas, when males talked about having a good time on the border, it usually meant visiting brothels on the Mexican side. That was something I had never done or planned to do.

Much to my relief, Jake decided to take the King Air, which meant that we would use the services of Albert, the company pilot. The contrast in flying technique between Albert and Jake was remarkable. Al had served in the Air Force during World War II and at the age of eighteen was the captain of a B-24 bomber, flying missions over Germany with a crew of eight men.

Now he served as the company pilot, and he never took chances. I watched him as he went through the preflight checklist. It was a procedure he had executed thousands of times, but he spent thirty minutes doing it, checking off every item as though he'd never done it before. Even though he had an instrument rating, he didn't fly into clouds and took no chances with Texas weather.

He flew that plane as though he was scared to death of flying, and that struck me as a sensible way to be a pilot. Once in the air, he didn't play chess.

In McAllen, Albert stayed with the plane while Jake and I joined up with a man we'll call Eddy Patterson, the main cattle buyer, and several of his friends. Eddy picked us up in his green 1966 Cadillac and took us to Sam's Restaurant in Reynosa, across the Rio Grande River in Mexico. We had a delicious meal: several courses of appetizers, then plates heaped with fried frog legs and roasted goat meat.

Eddy belonged to a class of men who made their living on the border, dealing in various commodities. Some traded in drugs, liquor, cigarettes, or migrant laborers. Eddy bought cattle and had to figure out how to get them through customs at the border.

During the meal, he told us that a Mexican customs agent had been murdered the night before in Reynosa, shot four times with a .45 pistol. The man who shot him had been transporting cattle across the border and had been giving kickbacks to the agent. Eddy's eyes and mannerisms suggested that he knew everyone involved and was concerned about it.

After the meal, we loaded into Eddy's Cadillac and drove to a darker, seedier part of town. Crossing a bridge that spanned a dry gulch, we came to a place commonly referred to as "Boys' Town." It consisted of a main street about five blocks long, lined on both sides with gaily painted, neon-lit fronts.

The street was full of holes, and the Cadillac dragged bottom on every one of them. As we drove along, men in white jackets stepped out and motioned for us to park in front of their place of business. Eddy ignored them. He knew where he was going and when he parked the car, he found an elderly man who was wearing a policeman's uniform and carrying a pistol. Eddy paid him to watch the car. I got the impression that they were acquainted.

Eddy led us into a bar that was clogged with men and women. A thin Mexican man with an alcoholic face sang to the music of a three-piece combo, while a girl danced, wearing the briefest of bikinis. When we sat down at a table, we were surrounded by women, most of whom seemed to know Eddy. Some wore wigs and heavy makeup. Others were young and pretty, someone's teenage daughter.

As the minutes passed, the men at my table disappeared into the darker parts of the establishment, until I found myself alone. A young girl sat down. She appeared to be fifteen or sixteen, had long black hair, a delicate face, and lovely dark almond-shaped eyes. I spoke enough Spanish to converse with her and asked where she was from. Yucatan. She asked if I wanted to go to a back room. I showed her my wedding band and said, "No, thank you."

That surprised her, and she stared at me for a moment. Then she said, "That's good." She smiled and walked away, swaying like a willow tree in a soft wind. Soon, she and a man vanished into the shadows.

PART 4

WRITERS AND WRITING

CHAPTER 14

READING AND STUDY

Six years in university settings had given me what we might describe as a pretty good liberal arts education. I had been exposed to great works of literature and had taken several writing courses, but when I began trying to write novels of my own, I confronted some questions—simple, basic questions:

> What IS a novel, after all?
> Is there some pattern or formula, and where might one find it?
> What is "good" writing? Is it a bunch of elegant words that you find in a thesaurus, words that most people never use? Is it dialogue? Long, detailed descriptions? Characters? Hidden references to mythology? Symbolism? Plot? A sociopolitical worldview?

During the years of my writing apprenticeship (1968–1984), I had a lot of catching up to do. In high school and college, I read what was required but didn't develop a love of reading until I left the university environment. I remember feeling emancipated. Now I could follow my curiosity and read anything that caught my imagination.

I began using my early morning hours for reading instead of writing. I read novels and short stories by Twain, Tolstoy, Dostoyevsky, Melville, J. P. S. Brown, Thomas Savage, Gore Vidal, Norman Mailer, James Jones, F. Scott Fitzgerald, Colleen McCullough, Arthur Conan Doyle, William Decker, Nabokov, Solzhenitsyn, and a number of novels by Herman Wouk.

Oftentimes, I tried to mimic the author's technique in my own stories and even attempted to draw "plot maps" on long sheets of newsprint. I recall charting *Tom Sawyer*, but my biggest project came with *Gone with the Wind*. It was a big book, and I used a lot of paper, tracing out the romance of Rhett and Scarlett.

What was the purpose of the plot maps? Well, I was an apprentice author, trying to figure out why one novel "worked" and another didn't, so I followed the procedure a biology student would use, dissecting a frog in a laboratory, studying guts and veins and muscles.

But dead frogs can't tell you anything about *life*, and that's what I was searching for: What makes a story vibrate with life? It seems ridiculous that I went to such lengths to answer a simple question, but it's the sort of thing an apprentice artist has to do when he's trying to learn his craft. Maybe there isn't an easier way of doing it.

Like most aspiring novelists, I had my fling with Hemingway. I admired his tight, muscular prose and the fact that he wrote out of his own experience, but I couldn't shake the feeling that his lead characters were hollow at the center. He had a pattern of bumping off the leading lady at the end of a story, which spared his heroes any kind of testing that might involve wedding vows or fatherhood.

I had great respect for Alexandre Dumas. *The Count of Monte Cristo* would probably rank near the top of my list of best novels. Its elaborate structure and moral content placed it almost in a class by itself, a near-perfect gem of the novelist's craft.

I read *Gone with the Wind* during my tenure as a bartender at the Perryton Club, usually late at night when two or three customers stayed late and denied me the opportunity to lock up and go home. Most literary experts don't have anything good to say about Margaret Mitchell and consider *Gone with the Wind* an example of lowbrow popular fiction.

I thought it was a great novel, and it didn't bother me that most Americans loved it. The toiling masses aren't always right in their literary judgments, but in this case, I think they were. It's a big story, well told. What more should we expect from a novel?

TEXAS AUTHORS

When Kris and I moved back to Texas in 1968, I discovered a category of literature that I had missed during my time as an undergraduate: Texas writers and writing.

When I was a student at UT, J. Frank Dobie was still on the faculty and teaching his famous course on literature of the Southwest. I knew his name and often walked past his house on Waller Creek. I even saw him on campus a time or two, but it never occurred to me that I should take his course or read his books. When I did get around to reading his books a few years later, I was amazed that such a literate voice was coming from a man who had grown up a ranch kid in South Texas.

I was busy trying to fill in the blanks in my education, which included just about everything written in Greek, Latin, German, French, Russian, and English since the time of Plato. For a pokey reader, that was a formidable task. Furthermore, it never occurred to me that Texas had produced books or authors worth including on my reading list.

At that time in my life, I had no strong sense of place or regional identity. Texas was something I wanted to hide or wash off, and one of the great disappointments of my life came when, after living two summers in New York City and two years in Boston, I realized that I had failed to scrub off the taint of being from Texas. I was stuck with a regional identity . . . and maybe it was important.

Living in Austin in 1968, I discovered the Texana section in Garner & Smith's bookstore on Guadalupe Street, and began acquiring and reading books by Texas authors, starting with J. Frank Dobie and J. Evetts Haley. I read *Blessed McGill* by Edwin Shrake; *The One-Eyed Man* by Larry King; *A Time and a Place* by William Humphrey; several books by an eccentric horse doctor named Ben K. Green; *Autobiography of a Durable Sinner* by Owen P. White; A. C. Greene's *A Personal Country*; and, in time, books by Larry McMurtry, Al Dewlen, Elmer Kelton, and John Graves.

I was surprised that Texas had produced so many good writers, and that many of them had come from little towns that were no more exotic than Perryton:

Dewlen—Memphis and Amarillo
Dobie—George West
Graves—Fort Worth and Glen Rose
Green—Cumby
Greene—Abilene

Haley—Midland and Canyon
Humphrey—Clarksville
Kelton—Crane
King—Putnam
McMurtry—Archer City.

I began to feel a kinship with Texas authors and studied their use of small-town settings and characters in their writing. In time, I met some of them, starting in the winter of 1971 when I learned that there was a published, practicing professional novelist living in—of all places—Amarillo!

CHAPTER 15

AL DEWLEN AND FOSTER-HARRIS*

I don't remember who told me about Al Dewlen. Maybe it was Mrs. Shanks, the lady who presided over the Perry Memorial Library across the street from the courthouse, or maybe it was Mrs. Love, my high school English teacher. At any rate, in 1971, someone in Perryton informed me that there was a genuine novelist living in Amarillo, one hundred twenty miles from Perryton.

He had a New York publisher, and his *Twilight of Honor* had won the McGraw-Hill Prize for best novel of the year. He had written another novel called *The Bone Pickers* that had whipped up a storm of controversy in Amarillo, yet I had never heard of him. I wanted to meet this guy.

*Portions of this chapter appeared as an essay in *Panhandle-Plains Historical Review* 39 (2018): 30.

Toward the end of January 1971, I was in Amarillo, looked up Dewlen's name in the phone book, called him out of the blue, and asked if I could see him. He told me to come over to his house at 4605 Matador.

The house was fairly large, a two-story or split-level affair in one of the suburban neighborhoods in southwest Amarillo. When I stepped inside the house, I saw a small fountain and goldfish pond, a large living room with modern furniture, a winding staircase that led to a loft, and a little poodle that barked at me.

Dewlen struck me as the kind of man who got lost in a crowd. In a room full of people, I wouldn't have picked him out as a novelist. He looked so . . . ordinary. When I arrived, he had been cleaning a deer rifle in the kitchen. We sat down at the table—round, marble-topped—beside a partition made of lava rock. He said, "What can I do for you?"

I told him that I was an aspiring writer from Perryton, and he started talking. For the first thirty minutes, his gaze avoided me. He would look here and there, around the room, as he talked. When he lined his face up with mine, he half-closed his eyes. It seemed an odd mannerism.

We sat there for almost three hours, and he did most of the talking. At all times, he showed courtesy and patience but always kept his distance. He was not a man looking for new friends or disciples. I didn't know it at the time, but two years before, he and his wife had lost their only child, a Marine who died in Vietnam. It had been a devastating blow and I'm sure he was still carrying the burden of it.

While he talked, I made brief one- or two-word notes to remind me of the subjects he discussed. (Interviewees are more at ease when they're not aware of an interviewer scribbling notes.) Later, back home, I made a long and careful entry in my journal book. It was a technique I had developed doing interviews for *Through Time and the Valley*.

THE DEWLEN INTERVIEW

Dewlen considered writing a teachable craft, not art. "Some people say that you learn to write by writing. That is baloney, if you'll pardon the expression. No one would think of saying that you learn to play the piano by sitting down and pushing keys. No one can teach you to write if you don't have talent to begin with, but if you have the talent, you can certainly be taught technique."

He had acquired his professional training at the University of Oklahoma's School of Professional Writing (SPW). The school opened in 1938, founded by Walter Stanley Campbell, Oklahoma's first Rhodes Scholar and a respected author who wrote historical nonfiction under the pen name Stanley Vestal. Campbell/Vestal was not your average English professor who taught imagery and symbolism, and from the beginning, his program aimed at producing professional writers, not scholars or teachers.

In the decades before television, a disciplined writer who turned out a five-thousand-word story every week could make a decent living writing for "pulp" magazines—so called because most of them were printed on cheap paper. Campbell himself never wrote for the pulp fiction market, but he hired a veteran writer who had published something like 800 short stories: William Foster Harris, who used the pen name Foster-Harris.

By the time I met Dewlen, the school had become a boot camp for writers and had turned out an impressive list of graduates: Louis L'Amour, Tony Hillerman, Mary Higgins Clark, Fred Grove, Bill Gulick, Bill Wallace, and Dewlen. L'Amour was one of the first students to enroll in the program and later appeared at the school "eight or nine times as a lecturer on writing the short story" (L'Amour 1990, 131). If memory serves me right, I once heard Elmer Kelton say that he took a correspondence course from the school.

Dewlen advised me to stop what I was doing, enroll in the SPW, and learn proper writing technique. It was sensible advice, but I couldn't see how I could make it work. Kris and I were as poor as snowbirds in winter, living in a tiny rental house and barely scraping by with my wages as a bartender-flunky at the Perryton Club. Furthermore, I had spent six years in college classrooms and had lost my appetite for anything that occurred on a university campus. I never wanted to spend another minute in a classroom.

Foster-Harris was still teaching at the school in 1971 (he retired in 1974 and died in 1978), and I missed my opportunity to meet him, but I did enroll in a correspondence course from the school and spent several months completing assignments and studying his *Basic Formulas of Fiction.* Foster-Harris believed that a good story placed two conflicting emotions into the ring and let them slug it out. A short story should solve a problem in moral arithmetic. "It is a parable depicting moral principles, just as in the parables of the Bible. Its basic pattern ordinarily is a simple arithmetical equation" (Foster-Harris 1944, 3).

My heart said that he was right in his essential arguments, but my mind couldn't accept his strict formulaic approach. Even so, I benefited from my study of Foster-Harris and would encourage any apprentice author to read his book. He gives us something to push against, even if we don't agree with everything he says. I probably absorbed more of his approach than I knew and worked out my own version of it later in the Hank the Cowdog books.

I asked Dewlen if he had any opinions about Larry McMurtry's novels. He said he had never "felt an urge" to read anything by McMurtry, then told me a story I hadn't heard before or since. He said that McMurtry's first novel, *Horseman,*

Pass By, was published the same year as *Twilight of Honor*, and both books became candidates for a cash award offered by the Texas Institute of Letters (TIL). *Twilight* had been a bestseller and a Book of the Month Club selection, while *Horseman* had enjoyed modest critical success but sold very few copies. The panel of judges gave the prize to Dewlen.

He heard the news when his agent called him from New York and asked if he was going to attend the TIL banquet in Dallas. Dewlen said no, he'd never had much use for TIL or any other writers' organization. The agent told him that he had won the prize, so he went.

When he arrived at the gathering, he found that people avoided him. "There was something strange about it." Come to find out, the committee—at least one of whose members had taught McMurtry at North Texas State—had held another meeting and had reversed their decision, giving the prize to McMurtry because "he needed the money."

Dewlen said, "I packed my bag and went home. That just goes to show you how those things work."

After my session with Dewlen, I made a careful study of his novels and developed a healthy respect for his approach to the writing of fiction. He was a fine novelist, yet today he seems forgotten everywhere but in Amarillo, where you still might find a few elderly residents who remember the furor *The Bone Pickers* caused when it came out in 1958. The characters were based on members of a prominent local family, and legend holds that they tried to buy up and destroy every copy in town. Their displeasure might have had something to do with Dewlen's decision to move away from Amarillo.

Dewlen might be the best Texas novelist that nobody has ever heard of. I learned a lot about technique, studying his novels. He died in Waco in 2011.

CHAPTER 16

HALEY AND GOODNIGHT

"All I know is what I've learned from a cow. I know no better teacher, none more honest and rigorous."

—J. Evetts Haley*

In the introduction to TCU Press's reprint of his novel, *The Time It Never Rained*, Elmer Kelton wrote about farm and ranch people in West Texas who have had to cope with the cruelties of drought.

> Traditionally it has taken a strong-willed, individualistic breed to live [in West Texas], especially when that living is tied closely to the soil, as is the case with the rancher and the farmer. Those not strong enough either

* From a speech delivered in Amarillo, Texas, to the Western Writers of America, June 1983. Portions of this chapter appeared as essays in *Panhandle-Plains Historical Review* (Spring 2014) and *Ranch Record*, Spring 2019.

> did not cross the line or retreated after being bruised by the demands of that uncompromising land. Those who remained became tough, resilient and almost militantly independent (Kelton 1984, x).

Kelton was attempting to depict Charlie Flagg, the central character of his novel, but he might just as easily have been writing about J. Evetts Haley. "Tough, resilient, and almost militantly independent" described Haley pretty well.

Haley grew up in Midland, Texas, where his father operated a hotel, a mercantile store, and a ranch in Loving County. He earned a bachelor's degree in history at the West Texas State Normal College in Canyon and in 1925 went to work as a field secretary for the Panhandle-Plains Historical Museum. In that position, he traveled around West Texas in a Model T Ford and interviewed hundreds of cowboys, ranchers, and pioneers, including the legendary Charles Goodnight.

After that, he studied for a master's degree at the University of Texas and spent seven years (1929–1936) on the faculty, where one of his friends was the noted author and folklorist J. Frank Dobie. But Haley wasn't an organization man. Stubborn, blunt, and opinionated, he didn't fit into the cultural/academic setting at UT.

After breaking off his friendship with Dobie, who was famously liberal in his politics, Haley left the university, returned to his ranching roots in West Texas, and set up shop in Canyon, Texas. There, he ran cattle on his JH ranch in Hutchinson County and wrote about the subjects that were dear to him. In time, he published his own books and eventually established a library and research center in Midland, the Nita Stewart Haley Memorial Library.

LONE WOLF HISTORIAN

Along the way, he invented a new career for himself, as a professional historian who was not affiliated with a university. England has had a long tradition of amateur scholars, usually clergymen, who pursued lifelong studies in arcane disciplines such as mathematics, astronomy, and Egyptology, but Haley, a young ranchman from Midland, had no such model.

Where would he have gotten the notion that he could pursue a life of scholarship without the facilities, companionship, resources, and respectability of a university community? How did he know that it might even be a possibility? It was quite a remarkable achievement.

In Canyon, he served on the board of the Panhandle-Plains Historical Museum, but that ended when he got into a feud with the board of directors and withdrew his manuscripts and artifacts from the museum. During the decade of the sixties, when most Texans were basking in the glory of having one of their own in the White House, Haley wrote and self-published a ferocious exposé of Lyndon Johnson, *A Texan Looks at Lyndon*. I didn't read it myself but heard that it accused LBJ of skullduggery on a grand scale.

Even people who didn't like Johnson found it bizarre. One critic described it as "bat-haunted." Larry McMurtry, for his part, called Haley "the Captain Queeg of Texas letters." When A. C. Greene reviewed the book for one of the Dallas papers, he dismissed it as "abominable." Outraged, Haley set up a press conference and roared his opinion that Greene was a "journalistic prostitute" (Greene 1982, 35). At the very least, the book was a departure from Haley's usual pattern of writing solid, scholarly works on ranch life and frontier history.

Haley was never loved by the keepers of Texas literature, but they couldn't deny that his biography of Charles Goodnight was an outstanding piece of scholarship, and every list of "best books" by and about Texans will include it. It's still in print more than eighty years after it first appeared. Dobie described it as "a full-length portrait, written out of fullness of knowledge. . . . It is the outstanding biography of the cattle industry of America" (Dobie and Dykes 1972, 5). A. C. Greene called it the best Texas biography he'd ever read (Greene 1982, 35).

Larry McMurtry considered the Goodnight book "the most impressive Texas book of the thirties" (McMurtry 1968, 51). "Despite his deeply reactionary politics, he was a brilliant historian and master of considerably more graceful prose than Webb's—or J. Frank Dobie's, either. Haley's biography of Charles Goodnight remains the single best biography of a cattleman—perhaps of a Western figure of any kind" (McMurtry 1999, 94).

AN INTERVIEW WITH MR. HALEY

In 1972, Kris and I were living in Perryton. I was following a disciplined pattern of writing every day and had begun to sense that *place* might be an important ingredient in my writing efforts. After reading the Goodnight biography and several other books by J. Evetts Haley, I wanted to meet him.

He was living in Canyon, fifteen miles south of Amarillo, and one day I worked up the courage to knock on the door of his stately Spanish-style home. Haley had a reputation for being a blowtorch of political opinions and meeting him required courage.

His wife Rosalind answered the door. She was his second wife, whom he married after the death of his first wife, Nita, in 1958. Rosalind was a beautiful, graceful, dignified woman, but she was suspicious of me. I got the impression that she screened her husband's appointments and had honed the skill of turning people away.

I told her that I was an aspiring writer from Perryton and the great-great-grandson of Martha Sherman. An account of her brutal murder by Comanches appeared on page 49 of the Goodnight book. I managed to win Mrs. Haley's trust, and she invited me inside.

When I entered the house, I noticed a leather holster attached to the inside of the door. It held what appeared to be a .45 Colt revolver. Maybe this was the normal precaution of a ranch-raised Texan, but later, I read that Haley feared that Lyndon Johnson would order reprisals against him for *A Texan Looks at Lyndon*.

I met "the Captain Queeg of Texas letters" in his book-lined study, and he disliked me on sight. I didn't dress "cowboy," because I wasn't one at that point in my life. Fresh out of UT and Harvard Divinity School, I wore longish hair and a defiant little shrub of beard, and he didn't approve of either one. He might have thought I was a student radical or a hippie.

I could tell that my appearance annoyed him. He remained civil but grumpy through two hours of conversation about writing and Panhandle history. He warmed up a bit when I told him about my ranching kinfolks in Gaines County and that I had been raised on stories about Tom Ross, the well-known outlaw who was convicted of gunning down two Cattle Raisers inspectors in the lobby of a hotel in Seminole. My ranching kin knew and feared Ross, and my mother had gone to school with his daughter, Bess.

Finally, old Haley couldn't stand it any longer. "John, you seem a pretty nice kid, but why do you wear those damned whiskers?"

I had been expecting this and had prepared a response. "Mr. Haley, after reading your book, I admired Charles Goodnight so much, I wanted to grow a beard, just as he did."

I don't know how many times in his life Haley had been caught speechless, but this was one of them. After scorching me with a glare worthy of Old Man Goodnight himself, he dropped the subject and made no objection when Mrs. Haley invited me to stay for lunch.

By the time I left, he had thawed enough to smile and wish me well and even invited me to come back. I give a full account of this encounter with Mr. Haley in *Prairie Gothic* (Erickson 2005, 48–56).

THE GOODNIGHT LEGACY

Maybe Haley's eccentricities, like those of Charlie Flagg, grew out of his ranching background in arid West Texas, but they also mirrored Old Man Goodnight, who was notoriously blunt, gruff, ill-tempered, and impatient with fools and neophytes. That included young Haley when he first approached Goodnight about doing a book about him. Here is Haley, describing his first meeting with Goodnight: "He was a very old man when. . . . I hesitatingly crossed his ranch-house yard to face the flow of tobacco juice and profanity, I reverently recall, which masked his most sensitive nature, and heard him explode with a lusty vigor against those writing such "a pack of lies about the West" (Haley 1949, ix).

I have wondered if Haley might have adopted some of Goodnight's mannerisms, consciously or not, simply out of reverence for a great man—and Goodnight was *that*, without question, a man of enormous will, courage, vision, strength, integrity, intelligence, and endurance; a trailblazer, explorer, fighter, entrepreneur, manager, innovator, amateur naturalist, and observer of all things within his field of vision.

If exposure to such a man left a permanent mark on Haley, we shouldn't be surprised, and I would suggest that the branding didn't stop there. Haley passed it along to his own generation, and then to the next and the next. When I read my grandfather's first-edition copy of the Goodnight book, I felt a strong kinship with the historian, but also a powerful bond with Goodnight.

Two of Texas's most distinguished writers, Elmer Kelton and John Graves, have written about the impact Goodnight had on their views of Texas, past and present. Graves said, "He was a tough and bright and honorable man in tough not usually honorable times" (Graves 1960, 62). Kelton wrote, "I am not the only one who has borrowed liberally from Goodnight. Ben Capps did it with his *Sam Chance*. Larry McMurtry did it in *Lonesome Dove*. I guess a lot of us owe some royalties to the Goodnight estate" (Kelton 1993, 290).

I think we can find outcroppings of Goodnight in the work of other Western artists and writers I have known and worked with over the years:

> Poetry: Baxter Black, J. B. Allen, Waddie Mitchell, Buck Ramsey, S. J. Dahlstrom, and Larry McWhorter
> Music: Rooster Morris, Red Steagall, R. W. Hampton, Chuck Milner, Michael Martin Murphey, Robert Vandygriff, Frankie McWhorter, Mark Erickson, Andy Wilkinson, Andy Hedges, and Don Edwards
> Visual artists: Ace Reid, Bob Moorhouse, Gerald Holmes, and Wyman Meinzer.

I would bet that every one of them owned Haley's book and considered himself touched by the Goodnight legacy. That is a remarkable testimony to the power of Goodnight's example and to Haley's role as a bridge between the Old West and the New.

Part of that legacy is that many of us who have tried to write and sing about the West exhibit some of the eccentricities of Goodnight and Haley. We tend to be "tough, resilient, and almost militantly independent," and we don't quite fit the mold of the corporate entertainment culture.

Most of those writers and performers have followed unconventional career paths, outside the shelter of universities, foundations, government agencies, and mainstream cultural organizations. Many of them had their fling with Nashville, Hollywood, or New York, and found that it lacked something too important to give away. Most of them, including me, were involved in self-publishing at one time or another.

John Graves described his own distinctive approach to writing as "archaic" and out of step with the times. I think there was more than a dash of "archaism" in Haley, and he laid out a pattern of writing and scholarship that went against the grain of accepted practice. He not only proved that it could be done, but that it could be done *well*.

After our first meeting in 1972, Mr. Haley and I stayed in touch and exchanged a few letters. He spoke highly of the articles I was writing for *The Cattleman* and *Livestock Weekly*—a great compliment, because he had deep knowledge of ranching and livestock and was a ferocious critic of anything that didn't have the smell of the fire. He admired my first book, *Through Time and the Valley*, and he should have. It followed a pattern he had laid out for authors like me. It was honest and well-researched. I did it the right way.

In 1983, the Western Writers of America held its annual convention in Amarillo. I was chairman of the program committee and invited Mr. Haley to address the group. He came in the company of Mrs. Haley and historian Byron Price and gave a stirring speech that earned him a standing ovation from the audience. One of the first to rise and applaud was Elmer Kelton, a writer Mr. Haley admired very much. So did I.

After the speech, I had a few moments alone with Mr. Haley and asked if he had ever met anyone who compared with Goodnight. "No, never. He was unique. He was a great man." That was the last time I saw Mr. Haley, and we parted with a warm handshake. I still had my damned whiskers, but he had forgiven me.

CHAPTER 17

ANDY WILKINSON: HISTORY, POETRY, AND SONG*

Andy Wilkinson, the Lubbock-based poet and musician, had a special connection to Goodnight, his great-great Uncle Charlie. Andy grew up listening to stories told by his mother and grandmother and played on a buffalo-skin rug the Old Man had given the family. In 1994, he published a book-and-CD set called *Charlie Goodnight: His Life in Poetry and Song*. It was, and still is, an extraordinary piece of work.

* Portions of this chapter appeared in *Ranch Record*, Winter 2022.

Haley looked at Goodnight through the lens of prose history, while McMurtry, Kelton, and Capps chose the medium of historical fiction. Wilkinson took a different approach: fifteen original poems and fourteen songs that followed Goodnight from his youth, riding a horse from Illinois to Texas, to his old age, sitting on a porch and thundering about the poor quality of town coffee.

Andy did extensive research on Goodnight, mining Haley's biography and other sources and adding his own family's stories to the mix. What's in the songs you could teach as Texas history, but he was also reaching for truth behind the historical facts.

It was a daring choice of media, poems instead of prose, songs instead of historical essays. In Goodnight's time, the Panhandle-Plains wasn't particularly fluent in poetry. We occupy a land of big horizons and straight lines, and our language tends to follow the geography. Goodnight personified that principle: his language was straight, blunt, unsubtle, and prone to storms.

You could make a similar point about our music: country-western, bluegrass, hymns, and folk songs. They tend to be simple and direct, not musically complex. Many of our tunes can be played with three basic chords. Andy's melodies retain that simplicity but incorporate minor chords and variations that add depth without intentional obscurity.

His songs send young guitar players back to their chord books to figure out what he's doing, and what he's doing is musically exciting.

If Goodnight ever wrote or read a poem, played an instrument, or sang a song, I haven't seen a record of it, and a sentence from one of Andy's songs confirms it: "He's not a singer, couldn't carry a tune / In his saddlebags or pocketbook" ("Song for Molly, Mary Ann"). He wasn't a poet or a musician, yet Andy chose to tell his story through songs and poetry. We don't know what the Old Man might have thought of the album, but I thought it was brilliant.

Andy's songs and poems don't just rhyme, they are built of sentences that deliver emotional content that speaks to every age about danger and courage, the vastness of the prairie, and the power of the wind. Other subjects touch the heart:

> "White Women's Clothes" captures the wrenching story of Cynthia Ann Parker better than anything I have read or heard.
> "Standing Deer's Lament" and "The Last Buffalo Hunt" tell about the other side of Anglo settlement, the tragedy of Native people locked out of what had once been their home country.
> "A Woman's Life" expresses an obvious but often overlooked fact of life on the prairie: it was a lonely place for a woman, listening to the never-ending moan of the wind and talking to chickens in the yard.

PERFORMANCE

Andy managed to draw some very talented musicians into these recording sessions, most or all of them from the Lubbock area: Alan Munde on banjo; Joe Carr on mandolin; Joe Stephenson on fiddle; Kerry Ford on harmonica; Andy on guitar; and Lloyd Maines on guitar, bass, dobro, and any other instrument they needed.

Singing talent included Buck Ramsey and Andy, as well as Lubbock's amazing Maines family: Lloyd, Donnie, Kenny, Brian, La Tronda, and Lloyd's teenage daughter, Natalie, who later became the lead singer with the Dixie Chicks. Her rendering of "White Women's Clothes" is unforgettable.

Not long after the album came out, I saw Andy at the National Ranching Heritage Center's Cowboy Symposium and gave him a torrent of praise. He smiled and said, "It's all Lloyd Maines. He did the arrangements." Well, it wasn't quite "all Lloyd Maines." Lloyd was an incredibly gifted musician who improved everything he touched, but he had something to work with. He took Andy's good musical concepts to a higher level.

Almost thirty years after I first heard the Goodnight album, I still consider it a masterpiece of Texas music and literature. It's so good, in so many ways, it leaves me thinking, "Let's just turn out the lights, lock the doors, and go home. There's nothing left to say." Coming from one author to another, that is high praise.

It also causes me to wonder . . . do school kids in Lubbock and Abernathy and Amarillo and Perryton even know it exists?

Those of us who grew up on the Llano Estacado have a tendency to define "culture" and "literature" as things that happened somewhere else, far from cow lots and cotton gins. It's a kind of regional inferiority complex and I've struggled with it myself. It arises, in part, from the absence or near absence of regional literature and music in our schools, which serve as definers and conduits of cultural material.

I hope that at some point in their school careers, our kids will encounter Andy's songs and poetry, because they're more than local history. Andy finds the universal in the particular, a whole galaxy in a raindrop, the story of all mankind in the lives of Goodnight, his wife, his cowboys, displaced Comanches, and poor, tragic Cynthia Ann Parker.

A whole galaxy in a raindrop. Gee, that's the kind of thing you'd expect to find in Real Art.

CHAPTER 18

JOHN GRAVES

In 1957, a young English professor set out on a canoe trip down a two-hundred-mile stretch of the Brazos River in North Central Texas and used the experience as a thread that connected a number of stories in one volume about local characters and events of historical interest. It was an odd book in that it jumped from present to past, and from history to fiction. It was neither a novel, an outdoors adventure story, nor a piece of historical scholarship. It was none of them, all of them, and more besides. The title simply read: *Goodbye to a River: A Narrative*, by John Graves.

I can imagine that the first editor who looked at the manuscript wondered, "What is this?" My own experience with the publishing world led me to suspect that Graves received some rejection slips that said, "This is too regional for us" or "We like this but don't know what to do with it." But Graves found a publisher, a good one, Alfred A. Knopf in New York. They brought the book out in 1960, and *Goodbye to a River* is often mentioned as one of the best books ever written by a Texas author.

I would second that, and so did critic/reviewer A. C. Greene: "*Goodbye to a River* alerts the reader, from page one, to the fact that this is a masterly work, worthy of almost any literary comparison. I rank it the finest piece of Texas writing ever done" (Greene 1982, 86).

By the time Graves wrote the book, he had traveled far beyond the Fort Worth of his youth. He served in the 4th Marine Division in the Battle of Saipan and lost an eye to a piece of shrapnel. By odd coincidence, my father served as a medical staff sergeant on that same island, probably around the same time. It is possible that he was working in the hospital where Graves received his first treatment. How strange it would be if their paths crossed in 1944 when I was one year old.

After the war, Graves lived in Spain, traveled across Europe, and spent time in New York City. He acquired an undergraduate degree from Rice University and a master's in English literature from Columbia. He was well traveled and well read, a man who had seen the best Europe and New York had to offer, but he went back home to write *Goodbye to a River*, a masterpiece that wore the rough garments of local history.

In his memoir, *Myself and Strangers*, Graves talked about the rediscovery of his roots.

> The years away from Texas, to my surprise, had accomplished something I had not anticipated or hoped for, allowing me now to return to home grounds and family and social roots and to see them whole. . . . They were entirely mine. . . . I had finally managed to discern some subject matter that was right for me, and, for better or

> worse, to attain my full voice as a writer. . . . It was a liberation, *Goodbye to a River* (Graves 2004, 231 and 233).

He created his own literary form and found a writing voice that was elegant, ancient, and poetic. Between snippets of local history, he quoted or ruminated upon the work of Shakespeare, Veblen, Thoreau, Hemingway, Juan Ramón Jiménez, Chaucer, Shelley, Yeats, Dickens, Trollope, Milton, and Cervantes, as well as the Bible.

Graves was searching for universal principles in his own backyard and aimed his story at readers who might not have been able to find West Texas on a map.

THROUGH TIME AND THE VALLEY

Until I read *Goodbye to a River* in 1969, I didn't even have the vocabulary to describe what my heart and instincts were telling me to do. Now, here it was! John Graves had already done it. He'd blazed a trail through the desert and had left a clear set of markers for those who came behind him. For me, an apprentice writer, it was an astonishing discovery.

In 1970, with *Goodbye to a River* as my pattern, I began doing research for a book about the Canadian River Valley in the northeastern Panhandle, a hundred-mile stretch of big, empty ranch country that had fascinated me when I was growing up in Perryton. Very little had been written about this area, so I had to do most of my research from scratch, interviewing cowboys, ranchers, and old-timers who supplied me with stories that very few people had ever heard.

In June 1972, photographer Bill Ellzey and I set out on a fifteen-day, 150-mile horseback trip that took us down the river valley. A treacherous pack mule named Dobbin lugged our bedrolls, a small tent, some dried food, a few extra clothes, and

Bill's camera supplies. This obvious imitation of John Graves's canoe trip on the Brazos gave me the thread that bound my stories together, just as Graves had done. At the time we made the trip, we hoped to sell the story and photographs to *National Geographic* magazine.

National Geographic wasn't interested, so I ended up making it into a book. I shopped the manuscript around and received a number of rejection slips, but finally got a hopeful reply from Bill Wittliff at Encino Press in Austin, a small outfit with a growing reputation and a strong list of Texas books. Bill sent me a contract and I was excited. Several months later, he had to withdraw his offer because of "problems" he was having with his printer. I expected to hear from him again, but we never got back together. It was a big disappointment for me.

In fall 1973 I drove down to Austin and met Wittliff, who was just beginning to make a name for himself in Texas publishing circles. Years later, he hit it big by writing the screenplay for *Lonesome Dove*. We spent a pleasant afternoon in his Encino Press office in an old mansion west of downtown Austin and later joined his wife Sally for supper.

Bill was very knowledgeable about Texas authors and literature and a great admirer of J. Frank Dobie, a personal acquaintance of his. He knew many Texas authors and I enjoyed hearing him talk about them. By that time, I had done a fair amount of reading of Texas literature but had met only a few authors.

It didn't take long for our conversation to focus on John Graves. I told Bill that *Goodbye to a River* had provided me with an example of how "regional writing" could transcend its region, and that I had gotten my design for *Through Time and the Valley* from Graves.

Wittliff not only knew Graves but was a good friend, and they stayed in contact. I pumped him for stories. I wanted to hear everything. He told me that Graves lived on a rough four-hundred-acre place outside of Glen Rose, south of Fort Worth, where he was in the process of building a two-story house with his own hands.

He said, "Glen Rose wouldn't be much out of your way when you drive back to the Panhandle. Why don't you stop and give him a call? Tell him I said the two of you ought to get acquainted." He gave me a phone number.

The next day around one o'clock, I drove into Glen Rose, stopped at a gas station, and called John Graves from a pay phone. I stammered out my story: I was a young author from the Panhandle, etc. He didn't exactly let out a groan, but his response let me know that he had other things to do and it wouldn't break his heart if I just kept driving. But I didn't let him off the hook, and at last he said, "Well, come on out," and he gave me directions to his place in the country. (I give a full account of this visit in *Prairie Gothic*.)

We had so much in common and shared so many interests, the afternoon flew by in a sweet cloud of conversation. Around six, John's wife Jane arrived from town with their two daughters. Jane was a New Yorker and at first struck me as rather stern and direct, but she liked me and invited me to stay for supper. I ended up spending the night on their couch.

The next morning, John went to his office in the barn, and Jane and I talked over breakfast. He came around to say goodbye, but I never doubted that it was time for me to go. He had enjoyed our conversations, but Graves followed a routine that involved work in the morning, not chatting with visitors.

BALANCE

After teaching several years at TCU, Graves devoted much of his time to making improvements on his place, which became the focus of his books *Hard Scrabble* and *From a Limestone Ledge*. Writing and reading in the early morning hours and doing physical labor the rest of the day, he created a balanced tension between book-knowledge and the practical wisdom that accrues to human beings who dig, sweat, build, observe growing things, and participate in the perpetual rhythms of animals.

After building a barn and a two-story house with his own hands, he set out to improve and restore his four hundred acres of rocky cedar hills, land that had been worn out by drought and poor management (overgrazing and too much cotton). He cleared cedar, moved rocks, planted grass and trees, and brought old springs back to life.

He raised chickens, goats, and cattle, kept hives of bees, and began to notice a feeling of kinship "with Sumerian farmers working in fields beside the Tigris and hearing from far off the clash and clang of mad kings murdering one another. . . . Old reality survives, blinking at you there, lizard-eyed. Survives and will prevail" (Graves 1996, 109).

The Hard Scrabble property became the drop of water into which he gazed and saw an entire universe. He described simple objects and events with prose that caused professional wordsmiths (often a hissing, jealous lot) to gasp in admiration. Here is Graves illustrating a commonplace event, the changes in the seasons:

> The seasons roll by toward wherever it is that they go: tawny wind-fanged winters give way to long lush springs, and summers with (perhaps) small sheeplike clouds riding above the southwest shove of searing Chihuahuan air finally yield to moist and melancholy and exultant falls with northers and high skeins of big birds trumpeting overhead (Graves 1996, 105).

I was impressed by his ability to occupy two worlds that were moving in opposite directions: city-country, urban-rural, university-agriculture, liberal-conservative, *Texas Monthly-Livestock Weekly*. I think Graves felt that a fully educated man should know both worlds.

He lived among country people, dressed as they dressed, was fluent in their blue-collar dialect, and could talk with them for hours about welding and range conditions, but he was anything *but* a redneck writer. His books were read and admired by the college-educated upper middle-class who lived in leafy suburbs that Graves had chosen to escape. His country neighbors might not have even known that he was a writer.

Somehow, he was able to maintain his sense of equilibrium. Literary Texans adored him and showered him with honors, but he never quite belonged to their world. Environmentalists saw him as a champion of their causes, but Graves had an understanding of nature that went deeper than politics. It included death as well as life, decay as well as growth.

Four months after meeting Graves, I took a job managing a ranch in Beaver County, Oklahoma, and began a seven-year odyssey, writing in the early morning hours, then doing my work as a cowboy. I had been offered the cowboy job before I met John Graves, so this turn in my life toward physical labor and solitude wasn't entirely an imitation of his example, but there is a striking parallel between the path I chose and the one I'd seen Graves pursuing at Hard Scrabble. It's a routine I have followed for more than fifty years, now on my own ranch in the Texas Panhandle.

I don't think it would be self-flattery to say that John Graves and I became friends, although it was friendship at a distance. He was a solitary man and, after invading his sanctuary on two occasions, I respected his privacy and didn't go back. Our circles sometimes crossed at literary events, though we were both so busy signing books, we had little time for more than a few words. I saw him and Jane at the Abilene Book Festival in 2003, and again at the Texas Book Festival in 2006. At the latter event, he was hobbling due to bad knees and using a cane.

Most of his friends called him John, but I could never bring myself to do that. It suggested a level of equality I didn't feel. He remained "Mr. Graves" to me, and that is how I addressed him in the many letters we exchanged over forty years.

My letters were longer than his replies, and his were often slow in coming, but he always answered. He was one of a small number of friends with whom I could share thoughts on a wide range of subjects that interested me, which included livestock, range management, prairie fires, literature, archaeology, weather, wildlife, philosophy, ancient civilizations, and the rewards and torments of being a writer.

One of our topics of correspondence had particular resonance for me. On March 12, 2006, the Panhandle wind was screaming straight out of the west, with gusts up to sixty miles an hour. Around sundown, our son Scot called from Amarillo and said that two huge fires were sweeping across the Panhandle and we had better figure out if we were in the path.

We drove out of our canyon to a high spot above the caprock. Looking south, we saw an unbroken line of fire from horizon to horizon. It continued burning, off and on, for the next four days, and I watched it from high ground on our place.

It turned out to be the biggest fire event in Texas history and for four days, I had a ringside seat to observe it. It burned over 900,000 acres of land and cost the lives of twelve people. On the third night, it jumped the Canadian River and came within a quarter mile of our east fence.

It made the national news and brought firefighters from Dallas, Midland, and as far away as Oregon. I knew our friends and relatives were concerned about us, so I kept a daily journal of the events I was observing and sent the notes out as an email. I didn't have an email address for John Graves, and wasn't even sure he had one, so I printed out a paper copy and mailed it to him.

A week later, I received his response. He said that my account of the fires was interesting and well written and that I should get it published, something I had not thought of doing. I sent it to Jesse Mullins, the editor of *American Cowboy* magazine who had written an article on me. Jesse liked the piece and ran it in the December issue. He also submitted it as a candidate for the Wrangler Award; to my surprise, it won Best Magazine Article of 2006.

John Graves was pleased when I told him. In 2021, Texas tech University Press published a book I wrote about wildfires, *Bad Smoke, Good Smoke: A Texas Rancher's View of Wildfire.* Graves would have liked that book and might have even felt some pride in helping me on my writing journey.

In 2006, the University of North Texas Press brought out my book *Prairie Gothic*, which contained a chapter about Mr. Graves. I sent him an autographed copy and he wrote back, "I love the book, lend out one of my copies (the uninscribed one) to people I know will return it, and urge others to buy it. In it you have captured a whole era and way of life" (letter to the author, June 1, 2006).

I also dedicated one of my Hank the Cowdog books to John and Jane. It pleased him, and he joked that the dedication caused him to "gain stature" with friends whose children were Hank fans.

My last communication from him was a postcard, dated March 12, 2012. He wrote: "I am still here, though not very active at nearly 92. Of course, I have lost most of my good friends by now, which makes your appearance via mail all the more welcome. Let's stay in touch, and I'll try to respond more fully to you next time. Cheers and best wishes—John G."

His response never came, and I assumed that his health was deteriorating. I was in Houston in August 2013 when several friends sent emails saying that he had died. The following day, the *Houston Chronicle* ran a story about him on the front page, an honor rarely bestowed upon an author. On the plane home, I noticed that the man next to me was reading a tabloid newspaper called *Texas Fisherman*. It, too, carried the news that we had lost a great writer.

John Graves touched many lives with his words. He certainly touched mine.

CHAPTER 19

HERMAN WOUK

One day I was horseback and rode upon a small group of cattle that were licking a spot of bare ground. I had never seen such behavior in cattle, and it took me a while to figure out what they were doing.

Years before, the rancher for whom I worked had put out blocks of salt on that spot, and though we no longer used it as a salt station, salt remained in the soil. The cattle were craving it and licking the ground to get it.

That episode describes my attraction to the novels of Herman Wouk: *Marjorie Morningstar*, *Winds of War*, *Youngblood Hawke*, and *War and Remembrance*. There was something in his writing that I needed and craved. What he was doing in his novels matched the literary theories I was struggling to develop on my own.

During the years 1974–78, while I was managing the Crown Ranch in Oklahoma, I set out to read everything he had written and made a serious study of his technique. For several years, he was my writing teacher. I read several of his novels in a pickup, as I waited for cattle to come to feed.

It's odd that I saw Wouk as a model and teacher, because we could hardly have been more different. Wouk was New York–raised, educated at Columbia University, an observant Orthodox Jew, a serious student of the Talmud, the grandson of a stern Yiddish-speaking rabbi, a scholar, a careful researcher, a student of history, and a reader of almost everything.

He spoke Hebrew and Yiddish, as well as French and probably some German and Russian, and studied the Talmud in Hebrew and Aramaic. He memorized a page from the Talmud every day. He read Spinoza and Maimonides and rabbi-scholars from the Middle Ages to the present.

He knew important people in business, movies, TV, science, academia, and the literary world, but those he most admired were rabbis and scholars, most of them unknown to folks like me but revered by obscure groups of men who wore black coats and funny hats. To him, study was a religious act. He said that when observant Jews greet each other, they say, "What have you learned today?" I have never known anyone who asked that question.

I sometimes consider myself a fairly serious scholar, and for rural Texas maybe I am. I write or study at least four hours a day. But Herman Wouk makes me ashamed of myself. I'm a crippled reader, too impatient to master any subject and too lazy to learn another language. I have trouble navigating Augustine in English, much less the Old Testament in Hebrew or the New Testament in Greek. Reading Wouk was always an enlightening but humbling experience.

What we had in common, I think, was a deeply held belief that a purely secular worldview will poison art at its roots. Wouk spent a lifetime grappling with a question that few authors even asked: *What is the author's function?* Is he part of the body of humanity, with an interest in maintaining the health of the whole, or is he a virus looking for a weakness . . . and a book contract and a movie deal and secular immortality?

Wouk didn't write "religious" novels, but his faith permeated all of his writing. "Religion and art both fight, on different fronts, against the dull rust that habit puts on the wonder of things" (Wouk 1987, 51). Over the years, I came up with my own one-sentence way of expressing this sentiment, which I passed along to young writers: "If you don't believe the first sentence in Genesis, I can't teach you anything about writing, because the whole process would be pointless."

I had a great deal more in common with Herman Wouk than I did with non-Jewish writers whose careless paganism drove me to despair. In 1976, I wrote him a letter, thanking him for being my teacher and for having the courage and wisdom to seek meaning in human experience. "Your novels are, to me, a lighthouse in a dark and stormy night. They are textbooks on what a novel should be."

His reply was an example of writing under exquisite control:

> At his opening night of *Arms and the Man*, when [George Bernard] Shaw took a bow and one lone boo was heard amid the applause, he said, "Sir, I agree, but what are our two opinions against so many?" In a reverse way your generous letter encourages my pleasantest fancies about my work. I get my share of kind letters, but few so eloquent and heartwarming. Thank you!

Wouk was a very successful novelist and playwright in the marketplace of American entertainment but also a man of enormous depth, a historian and philosopher, a scholar in the best sense of the word. His novels succeeded as literature and history, but on a deeper level, they showed Wouk exploring the mysteries of his faith.

He repudiated the nihilism and moral confusion of modern fiction, a view that was not widely held in literary circles during the 1960s and 1970s. He was one of the few popular writers who had the courage and stature to say it out loud and, of course, many literary critics regarded his thoughts as crude and lowbrow.

In 2010 I discovered two of his nonfiction books, *The Language God* and *This Is My God*, both serious works about Judaism. With Wouk, "scholarly" didn't mean impenetrable or pompous. "It is no service to a reader to load him with technical jargon to convince him that my words have weight. I have risked being as clear and pleasant as I could, and have worked very hard for clarity" (Wouk 1987, 7).

That was another lesson I learned from him, the importance of lucid prose. You might suppose that every practitioner of the craft would place a high value on clarity in writing, but that was far from the case. In some academic and literary circles, clarity meant simpleminded. If everyone understood what you were saying, maybe you weren't as brilliant as you thought. Wouk put that silly notion to rest.

In 2010, I wrote him another letter, thanking him again for his courage and wisdom and for being my teacher. I treasure his response:

> I've never received a more rewarding letter from a fellow author, a pleased reader of my work. You generously exaggerate my influence on your writings. If somehow my stuff struck a spark for you, that was lucky. . . . We all

> slog along and if the gift is there, sooner or later Becky Sharp, Hank the Cowdog, or Captain Queeg shows up to give us a place and a name. . . . I'm sending a copy of your letter to my editor, something I don't remember doing before.

I owe a large debt of gratitude to the rabbi's grandson, and my writing during the apprentice years showed his influence.

JOURNEY SONG

One of the qualities in Wouk's writing that impressed me most was his mastery of multiple points of view, entering the minds and speaking in the voices of different characters. The sweep of his imagination was stunning. He created point-of-view characters who were male and female, rich and poor, city and country, Jew and gentile, American and European, military and civilian, sophisticated and common. He even had the courage to enter the mind of one of the most enigmatic figures in human history: Adolf Hitler.

Inspired by Wouk's example, I spent several years trying to write a sprawling, big-canvas historical novel called *Journey Song*, set in Texas and Indian Territory during the administration of President Ulysses S. Grant. It dealt with the efforts of the federal government to pacify the Kiowa Indians, a culture of fierce nomadic horseback warriors, and to force them into living on reservations lands around Fort Sill.

The Grant administration's Peace Policy brought together three groups of people who seemed destined never to find common ground: the military, the Kiowas, and members of the Quaker church, who served as agents on the reservation.

I was fascinated by this period of history but had no special knowledge of it. To write about it, I had to acquire a small library of reference books, including a rare lexicon of the Kiowa language. I spent a year doing research and writing the first draft, which came to more than a thousand pages, and spent another six months editing, revising, and retyping the manuscript.

This was before the day of computers and word processors, so retyping a thousand-page manuscript—perfect copy, no mistakes, with one carbon copy—turned into a massive undertaking.

As usual, I thought it was a masterpiece. As usual, the editors at every major publishing house in New York didn't agree, and it brought me another harvest of rejection slips. They were very hard to take. Not only did they sink a dagger into my confidence, but to collect them, I had to drive eight miles on ranch roads to the mailbox, and eight miles back. It was a ritual I followed every day except Sunday.

Sitting in my pickup on the side of the highway, I would tear open the envelope and read the verdict, which usually began with, "We regret to say . . ." Then I would make the long drive back to the house and give Kris the report she had heard so many times before.

In 1983, Elmer Kelton, that wonderful, generous friend down in San Angelo, read my manuscript and took the time to write eight single-spaced pages of comments and editorial suggestions. He thought it was a strong story but too long. At its present length, it had no chance of finding a publisher. Following his advice, I did a thorough revision.

After several years, I quit sending out *Journey Song* and it remained in a dusty file drawer. In 2017, when my writing office was destroyed in a prairie fire, I thought I had lost the only remaining typescript and that it was gone forever, as well as my journals and letters from Herman Wouk. I winced at the loss but drew some comfort in knowing that what went up in smoke probably wasn't as good as I thought at the time.

But in the fall of 2022, I was poking around in an old file cabinet in a barn and was astonished to find a box of faded, brittle typewritten pages swathed in spider webs: the only surviving copy of *Journey Song*.

I was thrilled, as though I had discovered an old cedar chest in an attic, long gone and almost forgotten, that contained years of *me*—hopes, dreams, labor, pain, and pride. I dived into the manuscript and read it over a three-day period.

Was it as good as I thought back in 1976? Maybe. Maybe not. I was surprised that it didn't matter. I felt an odd sense of detachment from the book, as though it had been written by someone else. I remembered the author, that young man who was burning with ambition and trying to fight his way into the literary world but felt no desire to go back.

I had left that place, closed that door, and walked away. That's been a pattern in my life, closing doors and not going back.

CHAPTER 20

MARC SIMMONS AND LARRY MCMURTRY

MARC SIMMONS

In 1978, I took a cowboy job on one of the Barby ranches along the Beaver River in the Oklahoma Panhandle. Kris, son Scot, daughter Ashley, and I lived in a trailer house, thirty miles and thirteen cattleguards from Beaver City, the nearest town.

One evening in the summer, I got a phone call from a man named Marc Simmons, an author and historian from New Mexico. My first book, *Through Time and the Valley*, had just come out through Shoal Creek Publishers of Austin. He had read it and thought it was excellent. He was in the Oklahoma Panhandle, doing research on the Cimarron Cutoff of the Santa

Fe Trail, and wondered if he could drop by for a visit.

After taking a moment to absorb my surprise, I said, "Well, okay, if you can find me." He laughed and said he could. Sure enough, he found us the following day, at the end of a long sandy road.

Marc was a fascinating man: intelligent, competent, well-read, ambitious, opinionated, and as odd as a three-legged duck. He held a doctorate in history, had established a solid reputation as an author, critic, and scholar, and lived alone in the desert outside of Santa Fe. There, he had built a compound that included a house, barn, and a library of Southwestern literature that would have been the envy of most universities. All his buildings were constructed of adobe bricks, which he and a crew of men had made on the spot. He had no electricity, running water, or telephone, nor did he want them.

He had managed to cram a lot of living into his years. A teenager in 1954, he worked at a Christian mission in Arizona, lived among Navajo Indians, and tried to learn their language, which is extremely difficult for English speakers. (He failed.) He served for a while as a professor at the University of New Mexico, translated historical documents in Spain, and worked as a farrier, blacksmith, packer-guide, and cowboy.

He also wrote a regular column for the *Santa Fe New Mexican* and had become the unofficial arbiter in local disputes that involved anything historical. He loved getting into public fights with careless journalists, real estate developers, state bureaucrats, and politically correct professors. As an independent operator, he couldn't be intimidated or fired from his job, so his opponents were left with the unpleasant task of trying to beat him on scholarship.

With his enormous library and kerosene lamps that burned long into the night, he made sure they didn't.

Kris and I invited him to spend the night, and we stayed up talking, way past my usual bedtime. Marc and I had no trouble finding topics of conversation. We discussed ranching and cowboy work, Spanish iron and blacksmithing, the craft of writing, the declining standards of popular culture, Southwestern literature, and authors of the Southwest. He had met Conrad Richter, Tony Hillerman, Elmer Kelton, and many other writers, and I enjoyed hearing him talk about them.

I told him about the novels I'd been writing and about my many attempts to get them published. He advised me to write a nonfiction book about what I knew best and was doing every day (cowboying), and suggested that I contact a friend of his, Steve Cox, the director of the University of Nebraska Press (UNP). He said he would write a letter of recommendation.

I followed his advice and went to work writing *Panhandle Cowboy*, a book about my four years on the Crown Ranch in Oklahoma (1974–78). It was an honest description of cowboy work in the present day, written by someone who'd learned his stories on the back of a horse. It contained solid English prose and some good humor.

LARRY MCMURTRY

I sent the manuscript to UNP. They liked it, offered a contract, and brought out the book in 1980, with photographs by my friend and cowboy companion, Bill Ellzey. Larry McMurtry wrote the foreword, and people at the press were excited about that. I had mixed feelings.

I understood that I was a no-name nobody in the literary world and that McMurtry's name would give the book some respectability. He had become something of celebrity because three of his books had been made into movies: *Hud* (1963), *The Last Picture Show* (1971), and *Lovin' Molly* (1974).

In academic and literary circles, he was regarded as an expert on cowboys. He wasn't, but he'd grown up on a ranch and wore boots, so publishers paid him to write introductions for their books about the West.

He had the background to recognize that *Panhandle Cowboy* wasn't just another bowl of warmed-over hash, written by some library buckaroo, and in his foreword, he gave it modest praise: "*Panhandle Cowboy* is a sensitive, admirably straightforward book about the texture of modern cowboying in the Oklahoma Panhandle" (Erickson 1980, vii).

Actually, for McMurtry, that might have been more than modest praise. He wasn't much inclined to say nice things about Texas authors, but he was getting a paycheck from University of Nebraska Press, and they didn't hire him to throw rotten eggs at our new book.

When Kris and I moved back to Texas in 1968, I discovered his books and found that we had much in common. We both grew up in little West Texas towns that had never produced an author and we both had deep roots in Texas ranch life. His great-uncles had driven cattle up the Western Trail to Ogallala and might have shared campfires and adventures with my great-grandfather, Joe Sherman, who also made the trip.

That struck me as a remarkable coincidence. Even more striking was that both our kinsmen might have worked roundups and traded cattle with the uncles of Elmer Kelton, another small-town Texas author (Crane, Texas).

In 1969, when McMurtry was teaching at a college in Virginia, we carried on an exchange of letters. It was a friendly, lively conversation and he mentioned that he was working on a thousand-page novel, which might have been *Moving On* or an early version of *Lonesome Dove*. I wanted the correspondence to continue but it faded out.

Some of his writing touched me at a deep level but some left me sputtering in anger. I read his first eight novels and his collection of essays, *In a Narrow Grave*. I liked parts of *Narrow Grave*, *Leaving Cheyenne*, and *Horseman, Pass By* but had a bad reaction to *The Last Picture Show* and his Houston novels. I suffered through *Moving On*, one of the most boring novels I ever read, and quit him on *All My Friends Are Going to Be Strangers*. I couldn't stand another moment in the company of Danny Deck, a character who was as banal as his name.

McMurtry had a solid foundation in ranching and the traditions of the Old West, but there was a chord in him that never resolved. He loved the West but hated it. He wanted to preserve it . . . or maybe blow it up. At his best, he wrote vivid characters and expressed complex thoughts with the clean power of a lightning bolt. At his worst, he reminded me of a sullen teenager flipping lighted matches around the basement of his parents' home, not much caring if he burned it down.

Hollywood liked his novels. I didn't. *The Last Picture Show* struck me as angry, bitter, and shallow—Larry hoisting his middle finger at ranchers, cowboys, and small-town people, at his family and at mine too. In an essay written two decades later, he confirmed my impression: "It was the flattest and most hastily written of my books—dashed off, in fact, in a fit of pique at my hometown—and by the time it was published, I had ceased to think well of it" (McMurtry 1987, 18). Even so, it won the applause of an urban audience that already thought that small-town and country people were hicks.

For many years, I had a complex relationship with McMurtry's work. I rarely had a mild response to his writing, and the journals I kept between 1968 and 1980 contained pages of sincere praise and thunderous criticism.

I didn't read *Lonesome Dove* (I stopped reading fiction after

Hank the Cowdog entered my life), but my son Mark and many intelligent people have said it was a great novel, worthy of all the praise it received. There is no doubt that Bill Wittliff made it into a great movie, which I have watched many times. I am told that Wittliff's adaptation was very faithful to the novel

Here are some of Mark Erickson's comments:

> It is widely held that, in writing *Lonesome Dove*, McMurtry's purpose was to demythologize the West and the American Cowboy. May we all be grateful that he failed in this. From the moment Gus McCrae steps out onto the porch in the first paragraph until we say goodbye to Captain Call in front of the ashes of the saloon near Hat Creek, the book reads as one written by an author who loved his characters and subject matter, whether he wanted to or not.

It seems that *Lonesome Dove* contained none of the venom that I disliked in McMurtry's earlier books. Coincidentally, it was a smashing success as a book before CBS made it into a miniseries.

McMurtry was modest in his assessment of the book. He didn't consider it his best novel (*Duane's Depressed* was his favorite) and seemed almost scornful of its popular success. "What I learned from writing it was that myth is tenacious. Any attempt to demythologize the cowboy will only boomerang and end up striking whatever it attempts to debunk" (McMurtry 2009, 150).

In the 2020s, I read five of his nonfiction memoirs in which he talked about books, movies, and writing, and I thought they were good. Maybe he had mellowed. Maybe both of us had. My favorite was the one with the odd title *Walter Benjamin at the Dairy Queen*. It was the work of a deep-thinking, well-read man in the autumn of his life. He wrote at length about something he loved, buying rare books, and made some honest, illuminating observations about growing up on the ranch in Archer County and how it affected his view of the West.

> "I was a young cowboy who hated his horse and feared almost every animal on the place. . . . I was a reader, not a cowboy" (McMurtry 1999, 69).
> "I was involved in an act of escape: escape from the cowboy life, the life of men and horses, into the culture of books" (McMurtry 1999, 94).
> "In the American memory, the cowboy is mostly idealized. . . . Readers don't want to know and can't be made to see how difficult and destructive life in the Old West really was. Lies about the West are more important to them than truths" (McMurtry 1999, 55 and 62).

Another passage took my thoughts back to *Panhandle Cowboy*. McMurtry said that the publishers who asked him to write introductions for books on cowboy themes "were mostly shocked to discover that I didn't love cowboys and didn't want to wax poetical about them" (McMurtry 1999, 58).

McMurtry left the ranch, went to college, and immersed himself in books and literature. He *read* his way out of the Old West and, in his writing, set out to demolish the romanticized versions he saw in the books of J. Frank Dobie, Louis L'Amour, and others.

But the ranch kept pulling him back and he couldn't get away from it. For better or worse, that was his Place in the universe, "the geography" of his imagination, and to his great annoyance, *Lonesome Dove* became a permanent fixture in the literature of the romanticized West.

He didn't consider himself a scholar and, strictly speaking, he wasn't, but in his nonfiction books, he expressed strong opinions about movies, writing, poetry, literature, authors, books, and art. It was never clear to me what he considered the source of *value*, the qualities that made them good or bad.

If you follow a "good" book or movie to its source, what do you find? Is it good because it sells and generates income? Because it gets reviews and wins awards? Because it makes the reader/viewer better or wiser? Because it accords with a literary theory or fashion? Because it's honest and seeks truth?

But where do "truth" and "honesty" get their value, and who is defining the terms? Who says they're important and why should we care? Those questions point toward the non-material side of human existence, the side we often describe as "religious" or "spiritual." It was central to Herman Wouk's approach to the creative process. McMurtry showed no interest in it.

Did he recognize anything as Holy? Did he ever read a Psalm or say a prayer, and if so, to whom did he pray? He appeared to be a very secular man.

I met him only once, in April 1986, six years after the publication of *Panhandle Cowboy*, when we both participated in a symposium on Texas literature at Tarleton State University. *Lonesome Dove* had been a national bestseller and had just won the Pulitzer Prize for literature, and McMurtry was the headline speaker.

By then, I had published nine Hank books and nine solid nonfiction books on ranch life and cowboy work—the same way of life he was trying to debunk and demythologize. I had gained a following among cowboys, ranch families, elementary school teachers, and librarians, but was hardly known in academic or literary circles.

My invitation to the Tarleton event had originated with a professor in the English department, Tom Pilkington, whose children were reading Hank the Cowdog books in school. He had written several generous reviews of my books and had taken an interest in my self-publishing venture, Maverick Books.

McMurtry spoke to a packed house at seven o'clock in the evening and talked without notes for ninety minutes about Texas books and films. It was an excellent presentation. He had lost all traces of his Texas accent, if he ever had one, and spoke in a rich, strong voice with tones that seemed faintly British.

In my presentation, I talked for fifteen minutes about writing and publishing and read a passage from one of the Hank books. It went over well.

Later, at a cocktail party for faculty and speakers, I saw McMurtry sitting alone, sipping on a glass of water. He looked bored or tired. He had a head of thick, unruly dark hair that showed streaks of gray. He wore an old pair of black sharp-toed cowboy boots that had been polished many times and a herringbone jacket that was probably too warm for the season. One of the side pockets of the jacket had been machine-stitched with white thread, a careless job of tailoring by someone who didn't care about matching colors.

I went over and introduced myself, assuming that he would recognize my name. Why would he not? He was the man who knew everything about everything that had ever been written about Texas. We had exchanged letters, long letters. He had written the foreword to *Panhandle Cowboy*, and I had stirred up enough dust in the world of Texas letters to share a stage with him that evening.

He rose and gave me a firm handshake. I asked him how things were going in Archer County and he said things were bad, with the depression in the oil business. People were out of work and feeling glum.

And that was the extent of our conversation. He gave no indication that he had ever heard of me.

Maybe I shouldn't have been surprised. McMurtry had a reputation for cloddish behavior, so maybe there was nothing personal in it, or maybe he saw me as a rival. Professional jealousy is a common affliction of writers and I'm not immune to it myself. Our rancher-kin might have described it as "too many bulls in one pasture," the pasture being Texas Literature or Cowboy Mythology or some such.

My letters to and from McMurtry were destroyed when my office burned in the wildfire of 2017, along with the dozens of journals I kept during my apprentice years, so all of my ruminations about him, pro and con, went up in a big cloud of smoke. It's probably just as well.

He and I approached the West and storytelling in quite different ways, and I often disagreed with him, but I admired his courage and accomplishments. He was a disciplined writer and a gifted, intelligent man. At the end of his life, he held the attention of people in lofty places and became a towering presence in the literature of our time. Nobody from Archer City had ever done that before. It's rather amazing that he thought he could.

He certainly had an influence on my development as a writer and I regret that I didn't get to know him better . . . but maybe that is wasted sentiment. As John Graves once told me, "When people meet a writer, they're usually disappointed. The best of who we are goes into our books."

CHAPTER 21

WESTERN WRITERS

But back to 1978 and Marc Simmons' visit to our home on the Beaver River. He mentioned that he belonged to a group called the Western Writers of America (WWA). He suggested that I join and attend their annual convention in Boulder, Colorado. It would give me an opportunity to meet other writers, as well as editors and agents. Maybe I could find a publisher for the Western novels I had been writing.

I took his advice and joined WWA. Kris and I couldn't really afford the extravagance of attending a convention but felt it was something we should do. I loved my work as a cowboy, but my goal was to make a living as a writer. At the convention, maybe I would make contacts that would lead to bigger and better things in the writing business.

Up to that point, I had met only a few writers. At the Boulder convention, I met many:

Bill Gulick, a graduate of the University of Oklahoma professional writing school
Jory Sherman from Branson, Missouri
Jeanne Williams from Arizona
Spike Van Cleve from Big Timber, Montana
Ivan Doig from Idaho
Guy Logsdon from Tulsa
Jim Jennings from Amarillo
Don Worcester, Jane Pattie, and Judy Alter from Fort Worth
Elmer Kelton from San Angelo
Dale Walker and Leon Metz from El Paso
Don Coldsmith from Kansas
And a young novelist from California. I'll call him Jerry O'Brien and we'll see more of him later.

Spike Van Cleve and I hit it off well from the beginning. We were the only people at the convention who actually made our living in the cattle business, I as a cowboy in Oklahoma and he as a third-generation rancher in the Crazy Mountains of Montana.

Spike had short legs, thick shoulders, and a prosperous belly that hung over a belt buckle made of silver. His face was dominated by a hawk nose, a broad smiling mouth, and twinkling eyes that expressed energy, mischief, and a boyish sense of humor. He wore Western-cut pants and shirt and a straw hat whose brim had been reshaped, pulled down in front and back.

Loud, brash, and funny, Spike thought of himself as a rancher, not a writer. I never saw him at another WWA convention and

I'm not sure he was even a member, but his first book, *40 Years' Gatherin's*, had won a Spur Award and he'd come to accept it at the awards banquet. It was a fine book.

I also found a great deal in common with Elmer Kelton, the associate editor of *Livestock Weekly*. I had become a regular contributor of humorous stories to his paper but had never met him. Elmer's reputation as a first-rate novelist was beginning to grow, and he was regarded as one of the group's brightest stars. Thirty years later, they voted him the Best Western Writer of All Time. I'll say more about him in chapter 22.

LOUIS L'AMOUR

The Western author who *didn't* make an appearance at the convention was Louis L'Amour, who had sold more books than all the rest of us combined. I heard some members grumbling that he never bothered to come to the conventions. To me, it seemed a sensible course of action.

The rest of us attended conventions to chase editors and agents around hotel lobbies in hopes of getting something published. L'Amour had sold something like a hundred million books. What did WWA have to offer him? Nothing that I could imagine.

I had several friends who had read every book written by L'Amour and spoke his name with reverence. They were not what you would call bookish people. They didn't spend much time in bookstores and had no interest in the opinions of critics or reviewers, but in their homes, they had entire shelves packed with worn copies of L'Amour's Bantam paperback novels.

Given my background as a man of the West, I should have been an enthusiastic reader of L'Amour's novels but somehow wasn't. At the urging of friends, I read several of his books but never found whatever it was that had turned them into devoted fans. True, he was scrupulous about the details of location, clothing, food, firearms, and local customs, but his writing seemed rather bland, lacking the wit and quiet elegance of Elmer Kelton's prose.

Larry McMurtry was no admirer of L'Amour, whom he described as "the industrious pulper who spent a good part of his life hoping that people would mistake him for a realist" (McMurtry 1999, 58) but I had great respect for L'Amour's commercial success and his remarkable ability to transform nonreaders into readers. Years later, when I was out on the road selling Hank the Cowdog books, I considered it a great compliment when a customer said, "My husband doesn't read anything but Louis L'Amour and Hank the Cowdog." L'Amour might not have appreciated the association, but I did.

I never had the pleasure of meeting L'Amour but did get to see him two years later at a WWA convention in Santa Rosa, California, when he came to a banquet to receive a Lifetime Achievement Award. I felt certain that he came, first, because he didn't have to travel far to get there (he had a home in California) and second, because it might have seemed petty if he had told the WWA convention committee the truth, that he didn't need their award or approval.

So he did his duty and collected his plaque, and for an hour and a half, three hundred writers and would-be writers got to look at the man who had sold a hundred million mass market paperback books to truck drivers, cowboys, welders, dozer jockeys, lumberjacks, rig hands, windmillers, cedar-choppers, cotton-pickers, construction workers, and harvest hands.

I sat near the back of the banquet hall, but even at a distance, I could sense the power of his personality. He might have been an author for the common man, but there was nothing common about his appearance. He was eighty years old but looked stout enough to chop a cord of wood. He showed few signs of age or wear. He had deep, dark, piercing eyes, a broad face with apple cheeks, and thick chest and shoulders. Whatever one thought about his books, he came across as a man of integrity and strength.

His presence at the banquet was a triumph for WWA and a decent gesture by L'Amour. He was kind enough to lend his radiance to a group that had nothing to do with his success and to tiptoe past the fact that WWA had never given him one of their Spur Awards for Best Western Novel of the Year. (For what it's worth, between 1978 and 1985 I entered seven novels and nonfiction books in the Spur competition and didn't win one either.)

L'Amour's editor from Bantam Books, Irwyn Applebaum, attended the WWA convention in Boulder, and I managed to spend a few moments getting acquainted with him. It wasn't easy to seize a quiet moment with Irwyn. Among the cadre of New York editors who had come to the convention, he was probably the most sought-after by starving authors.

Irwyn could hardly have looked *less* like an editor of novels about the American West. He was a native New Yorker, Jewish, scholarly and dry, had small hands that reminded me of flippers, wore glasses and a thin reddish beard, and made no attempt to dress "cowboy" or Western.

I'm sure he wasn't impressed with me, nor should he have been. I was one of dozens of nobodies at the convention who burned with the desire to be the next Louis L'Amour. Three years later, after I had published several books, I had more conversations with Irwyn, as we shall see.

After the convention, Kris and I drove back to Texas. I returned to my cowboy job on the Beaver River and continued my pattern of writing four hours every morning in John

Little's barn. I had made a few contacts with New York editors, met some writers, and come home with some new ideas about writing Western novels.

It appeared that my future might lie in this direction, figuring out how to write Western novels that some editor in New York would publish.

CHAPTER 22

ELMER KELTON*

When I met Elmer Kelton at the WWA convention, he reminded me of my great-uncles, Roy and Bert Sherman, who cowboyed and ranched around Seminole, Texas. He and my uncles were shy in public and spoke in soft tones. They wore the same kind of rimless glasses that gave their faces an ascetic cast. Through the lenses of Elmer's glasses, one glimpsed the shocking clarity and depth of his eyes.

Like my uncles, he practiced a parsimony of language, dealing out his words like a poker player who had money riding on every card, and he and my uncles had the same rancher/cowboy sense of humor: sly, understated, and collateralized by a lifetime of careful observation.

My uncles were fluent in that approach to humor. Kelton was an absolute master of it.

*This chapter appeared in a slightly different version in *American Cowboy*, August 2014.

Elmer and I came from the same breed of people. At one time, Buck Kelton, Elmer's dad, worked on the Five Wells Ranch in Gaines County. My grandfather, great-grandfather, and great-uncles ranched in Gaines County. That was a small world, and it's likely that our kinfolks crossed paths.

If they were acquainted, they probably met once every five or six years, talked for fifteen minutes about family, grass, and rainfall, and went on their way—never doubting that the other party could be trusted with a sack of gold, a herd of cattle, or another man's daughter. They were, to use the cowboy expression, "good men to ride the river with."

That kind of bedrock honesty was built into all of Elmer's writing. He had an unspoken bond with his audience that he would never tell them a lie. In ranching circles, that has been accepted practice for a century and a half, but it's not so common in the world of publishing and entertainment.

There is a kind of inertial force at work in artistic fields that pulls them toward dishonesty. Sometimes it's motivated by money-lust or political correctness, but the most common source might be simple laziness: It's always easier to repeat accepted verities than to seek out and test truth every day.

Elmer sought out and tested truth every day. He read the work of other writers but also did his own research. He used his own eyes and ears and measured the results on his own internal set of scales. Those scales were calibrated by his experiences in West Texas, and they reflected the values of the communities where he lived and worked.

Over the years, Elmer and I exchanged letters and visited at conventions of the Western Writers of America. He contributed some funny stories to my biography of Ace Reid, whom he knew well and whose artwork he admired. I was honored that Elmer wrote the foreword for *Prairie Gothic*, where he said, "[Erickson] makes us feel the emotions of the many characters he brings to life. Some are happy, some sad, some simply frustrated, but all are engaging" (Erickson 2005, xii).

We knew each other for twenty-one years, but it was an odd kind of friendship. I never set foot in his house, nor did he in mine, and we never talked on the phone. I saw him at WWA conventions and later at book-and-author affairs in Abilene, San Angelo, Austin, Amarillo, and Lubbock, but our conversations rarely lasted more than ten or fifteen minutes. We talked about family, rainfall, and grass conditions, and that was about it.

It used to bother me that we had so little to say to each other, but I finally figured out that we didn't need to talk. There was nothing I could tell him about myself that he didn't already know. In typical rancher fashion, he had sized me up in his own way and had figured out that I was an honest man, worthy of his respect. I had done the same with him.

His father, Buck, foreman of the Jigger Y ranch in Crane County, and my great-uncles in Gaines County, had used that same method for judging cowboys, cattle buyers, horses, and friends. They learned what they needed to know and burned up very few words in the process.

AMERICAN NOVELIST

Elmer built his literary reputation one brick at a time, without advertising or public relations hype, and it was a slow process. He started out writing short stories for the "pulp" magazines. From there, he moved into writing mass market paperback Westerns, then to hardcover Westerns that won enough awards to stagger a packhorse.

Somewhere along the way, he ceased being a "writer of Westerns" and became an American novelist. At the time I met him, I hadn't read any of his thirty or so novels. I had never been an admirer of Westerns. Those I had read seemed shallow, predictable, and a bit silly, like the innumerable Western movies I had seen as a boy in Perryton.

When I finally got around to reading *The Time It Never Rained*, I was astounded by how good it was. Every word, every sentence, every line of description was a work of high craftsmanship, the book as a whole a quiet masterpiece. Reading it, I wasn't sure whether I should stand up and cheer or weep because I hadn't written it myself.

The original publisher, Doubleday, let the book go out of print, and wise heads at TCU Press snapped up the rights and brought out a new edition in 1984. Judy Alter, director of the press, asked if I would write a few lines for the back jacket. I said I would be honored. I wrote: "*The Time It Never Rained* is not just one of the best novels ever written by a Texan. It is one of the treasures of American literature of any age or time. Our great-grandchildren will still be reading Elmer Kelton."

THE GOOD OLD BOYS

The Time It Never Rained was a great novel, Elmer's personal favorite and the favorite of many of his loyal fans, but I was even more impressed with *The Good Old Boys* (1978). As a working cowboy, I had glimpsed the world of Hewey Calloway, the story's lead character, and with that perspective, was able to examine every detail of Elmer's story on a microscopic level.

There wasn't one false word or counterfeit emotion in the entire book. I doubt that anyone has ever written, or will ever write, a better, deeper portrayal of the American cowboy. Elmer understood the lure of manly adventure, the wild exhilaration of matching wits and physical strength against horses and cattle and weather, but he also understood that the cowboy's story often has a sad ending.

When Hewey cancels his engagement with Spring Renfro and rides off with cowboy pal Snort Yarnell (what a great name for a bachelor cowboy!) on another wild adventure, those of us who have lived Hewey's life, or who have loved someone who did, are gnawed by an uneasy feeling.

On the next-to-last page of the book, Hewey is about to ride away and has this exchange with his young nephew, Tommy. "Tears had cut a trail down Tommy's face. He put his arms around Hewey's neck and hugged hard. 'You'll be back, won't you, Uncle Hewey? You ain't goin' to let some old bronc kill you?'"

Hewey says, "Button, I ain't never been killed in my life."

That perfect diamond of a sentence captured not only the swagger of Hewey's approach to life but also its loneliness. We suspect that he will eventually find a horse that kills him or that he will spend a sad old age cleaning spittoons in a pool hall in some little West Texas town, telling his stories to eye-rolling teenage boys who have no way of understanding who he used to be.

When I heard that Elmer had sold the movie rights to *The Good Old Boys* (made for TV in 1995), I was happy for him and wrote him a letter of congratulation. But I was also worried. It often happens that a good book suffers the fate of being translated into a bad movie. Al Dewlen considered the film version of his *Twilight of Honor* one of the worst movies ever made.

I didn't think there was a writer, director, or actor in Hollywood who could preserve the honesty of Hewey Calloway's story in the film medium. I was wrong. Tommy Lee Jones played the lead role, co-wrote the screenplay, directed the film, and succeeded in capturing the integrity and depth of Elmer's story. From start to finish, he was attentive to the objective reality that shaped all of Elmer's work, a powerful sense of *place*.

Elmer was never comfortable with aesthetic systems that played fast and easy with the facts. No doubt this reflected his training as a professional journalist, but it had a deeper source: he was the son, grandson, and great-grandson of ranchers, people who came from *somewhere* and were rooted in *something*.

To him, *place* was not a snapshot of pretty scenery. It was a swirl of complex emotions and relationships that accrued to people whose lives were shaped by one specific patch of soil, and by the elements of nature that dispensed blessings and curses upon it. In Elmer's novels, place wasn't incidental or optional. It was an incubator of truth.

Tommy Lee Jones understood this and protected Kelton's vision through the process of translating written words into visual images. His attention to detail is breathtaking, and the film doesn't contain a false word or scene. The result is a great movie. I have watched it at least thirty times, and it gets better every time.

I have never read a list of "best" Western movies that even mentioned *The Good Old Boys*. To me, that is a stunning omission. If *The Good Old Boys* isn't the best Western movie ever made, it surely ranks in the top five. When Jones delivers Hewey's line at the end of the film, "Button, I ain't never been killed in my life," it brings mist to my eyes.

LITERARY FAME

As a young writer, I made a careful study of Elmer Kelton and the way he conducted himself as a producer of cultural material. I came to the conclusion that he could have sold a lot more books and made a lot more money if he'd cut a few corners, blurred a few lines, and lowered his standards just a bit.

But he didn't. He found the kind of fame he wanted, and it took him a whole lifetime to collect it. Along the way, he "kept his day job," as he often described it, working as an agricultural journalist: fifteen years as farm and ranch editor for the *San Angelo Standard Times*, five years as editor of *Sheep and Goat Raiser* magazine, and twenty-two years as associate editor of *Livestock Weekly*.

It always amazed me that Elmer could write all day about livestock markets and range conditions, then write novels at night and come up with stories that were not merely passable but good. I couldn't have done it, but Elmer had honed the process down to a sharp edge.

His day job not only kept him in constant contact with characters and story material for his novels but also gave him a good reason to say "no" to people with money, influence, and cheap ideas. Since he already had a job, he didn't need their money.

Elmer was never seduced by the literary trends that steered the American novel toward darkness and absurdity. He charted his own course. It wasn't glamorous, just honest. And he was revered by the people in his own region—a great and rare accomplishment for a novelist. Glenn Dromgoole, an Abilene bookstore owner and book reviewer, said he'd never known a writer who was as loved by his readers. "People would come in for a book signing, and it was like they were coming in to see a good friend."

When Elmer died in August 2009, I lost a good friend. I knew his wife and two sons. I autographed Hank books for his grandchildren, and he signed and personalized his books for me. He was always generous and encouraging.

Whether we remember Elmer through his art or his life, he was a good man to ride the river with.

PART 5

FINDING A VOICE

CHAPTER 23

THE COWBOY YEARS

In December 1974, I took a job managing a ranch in Beaver County, Oklahoma, and from January 1974 until July 1981, I made my living with a horse and a rope, working as a cowboy on three outfits.

During the spring and fall roundup seasons, I spent long days in the saddle, swapping out work with the neighbors and riding with big crews of men. I never talked about the six years I had spent in university settings and got no free pass for being an author. Nobody on the crew knew about that part of my life or would have cared if they had. I had to measure up to the standards of men who did nothing but ride, rope, and handle livestock and were very good at it.

This gave me a perspective on ranch life that was different from the one that informed the work of Elmer Kelton, Larry

McMurtry, and J. Frank Dobie. They were born into ranch life but were bookish, never acquired the skills of their fathers and uncles, and never drew a paycheck as a hired hand. I was town-raised, chose the profession, and had to master the skills.

I was never the best cowboy on a crew but was good enough to ride with them, and proud of it. The books I wrote were based on hard-won firsthand experience.

After the seasonal work was done, I always managed get back to the writing schedule that seemed to fit my needs and temperament: up at 4:30 or 5:00, write until 8:30, then do ranch work the rest of the day.

I had read about authors who wrote eight hours a day and tried it myself in the late sixties. I found that four and a half hours was my limit. Anything I wrote after that showed fatigue, and I seldom accomplished anything in the afternoons. When I was trying to write eight hours a day, I developed a whole repertoire of stunts and devices that kept me from doing anything productive: prowling around the house, staring out windows, whittling, and reading magazines, encyclopedias, and dictionaries.

Common sense finally intervened and pointed out the obvious, that I was wasting half my time. Working at a regular daytime job on a ranch actually improved my writing because it forced me to make wise use of my time.

I have written a number of nonfiction books about my cowboy experiences, and if I may say so, they remain solid, accurate, honest descriptions of what one cowboy did, saw, and felt in his time and place. Very few people know those books, but that body of experience played a major role in preparing me for my ultimate job as the creator of Hank the Cowdog.

It is hard, maybe impossible, to explain the creative process and to say with any certainty where a character or story comes from. It's more alchemy than science, a very mysterious composting of people and events that somehow yields something unique and delightful.

An analysis of my artistic compost heap would reveal several elements (my parents, my wife, growing up in a small town, my early religious training, a close association with dogs, exposure to oral-tradition storytellers such as Henry Gordon and Frankie McWhorter), but my involvement with ranch life would stand out as one of the most powerful. It pulled my mind out of books, away from myself, and showed me the living, breathing reality of earth, sky, and weather, muscle, sweat, and blood. It provided me with characters, both human and animals, and their voices. It gave me stories to tell, inside a tradition that had preserved the art of passing them along in humble settings.

LIVESTOCK PUBLICATIONS

In 1976, my writing took a turn. Though I continued writing novels and sending them off to New York publishers, I began composing short humorous articles for three publications to which I subscribed: *Livestock Weekly*, *The Cattleman*, and *Western Horsemen.* Copies of these periodicals were sitting around my house, yet I had been slow to grasp a simple truth: you should write for publications you already know and read.

I suspect that pride prevented me from seeing this fundamental concept. I had wanted to make my mark in big-time literary journals, not in cow and horse periodicals published west of Manhattan, but a steady stream of rejection slips finally changed my mind. I began sending articles to Stanley Frank at *Livestock Weekly* and to Paul Horn, the editor of *The Cattleman.* They liked my work, and I became a regular contributor to both.

In 1977, I talked Paul Horn into buying a series of stories that ran under the name "Alkali County Tales." These stories featured a grouchy rancher named Willie Onthenextranch and an eccentric animal scientist, Dr. Barley McOatwheat, who presided over a little agricultural experiment station in a backwater region of the American Southwest. Under the watchful eye of his secretary, Miss Mattie Sparrow, Dr. McOatwheat carried on a goofball crusade to make cattle-raising a profitable venture.

The Alkali County Tales were funny and resonated with readers who had known characters just like Willie and McOatwheat, but the most important feature of the series—to me, at least—was that Paul Horn allowed me to write *fiction* in a magazine that didn't publish fiction. I don't remember that Paul ever mentioned this, and I kept my mouth shut. Whatever his reasons, he gave me the opportunity to incorporate regional themes and local characters into a medium that had almost vanished in Middle America: the short story.

By the spring of 1978, I was churning out articles for livestock publications but still trying to branch out into Western novels. I had left the Crown Ranch and had taken a job on another ranch in Beaver County, Oklahoma. Kris and I and our two small children (Scot and Ashley) were living in a trailer house near the Beaver River, a hundred ninety miles from the Amarillo airport and thirty miles from the nearest town.

For two years, I did disciplined writing in a corner of John Little's barn and, for a while, it was a good place to be a writer.

SHOAL CREEK PUBLISHERS

On one of my many trips to the mailbox—it must have been in 1977—I received a letter from Luther Thompson, the owner of Shoal Creek Publishers, a small regional press in Austin. I had sent him the manuscript of *Through Time and the Valley.* He liked it and I was ecstatic.

I had started doing research for that book in 1970 and finished writing it in 1972. In the five years since, I had shopped it around to every publishing house I could think of and had collected the kind of rejection slips I had learned to dread and despise: "Too regional. Not quite right for us."

I became so discouraged, I offered to *give* the book to the Perryton newspaper, if they would print it as a serial story. When the editor turned me down, I felt that I had hit the absolute bottom. When the local paper won't run your book for free, you have become a leper in the literary world.

Shoal Creek Publishers consisted of a young editor named Judy Timberg and the owner-publisher, Luther Thompson, a tall, dignified gentleman in his seventies. Both of them admired my book, but Mr. Thompson, like so many editors and publishers before him, feared it was "too regional," even for his small operation.

I sent him a long, pleading letter, pointing out that while West Texas wasn't heavily populated, we did have a few people who could read. We had indoor plumbing and libraries and a few bookstores in Amarillo and Lubbock. Furthermore, I had established a modest reputation writing funny stories for livestock publications, and I thought we could sell enough copies of the book to make it worth his time and investment.

With a heavy heart, Mr. Thompson sent me a contract and the book came out in the spring of 1978, while I was cowboying in Beaver County, Oklahoma. The following August, when he sold out his first printing and ordered another, Mr. Thompson admitted that he was surprised.

Through Time and the Valley wasn't the first book I ever wrote, but it was the first to survive the vetting of editors and publishers who were unanimous in their judgment that any book set in the Panhandle had no relevance to readers anywhere else. The book has never been a big seller, but it remains in print today (University of North Texas Press) more than half a century after I wrote it.

It's a solid piece of work that has endured the test of time. It's not as good as the book that served as its pattern, *Goodbye to a River*, but it has never brought any shame to the writers who inspired it, John Graves and J. Evetts Haley.

CHAPTER 24

BACK TO PERRYTON

By the summer of 1979. Kris and I had been living on ranches in Oklahoma for five years. I loved my cowboy work, but it paid so poorly that we were perpetually broke.

I was writing humor articles for *Livestock Weekly*, *The Cattleman*, and *Western Horseman*, and that brought in a few extra dollars, but they always flew out of the checking account to pay for groceries, shoes for the children, and repair bills on our poor, road-beaten Ford Pinto.

Poverty is the dark side of the cowboy profession, and sometimes cowpunchers wake up to the fact that they've become indentured to the ranch. They can't afford the down payment on a house in town, can't cover the cost of moving, can't take days off to go looking for another job, and if their car is broken down, as our Pinto usually was, they can't even leave the ranch.

That describes our situation in the summer of 1979. I was locked into a job that paid five hundred fifty dollars a month and trapped on a ranch that was thirty miles from town. I was still years away from making any kind of decent money with my writing and our prospects looked grim. To make things worse, in August I injured my back in a horse accident.

Enter my father, Joe Erickson. On the phone one night (it was my good fortune that our quirky party-line rural phone system happened to be working), I told him about our plight. After a brief pause, he said, "You know, I've got a rental house that's vacant and it's about the right size for you-all. I'll give you the equity and you can take over the loan."

Yes, but my back was messed up, I couldn't lift boxes, and we couldn't afford to hire a truck to move our things. "Oh, that shouldn't be a problem."

That was the kind of thing my father did many times over the years—helped us without stepping on my pride. Yes, I was a proud young man, proud beyond a considerable body of evidence that said I shouldn't have been. I was too proud to ask for his help, but at the right moment, when he figured I'd had enough, he stepped in and gave me a hand up.

I found a job working on the LZ Ranch, south of Perryton, and we moved into a house in Perryton that any starving writer or cowboy should have been thrilled to obtain. I felt caged, living in town, didn't like the neighborhood, and hated the dog next door, but in lucid moments, I knew we were lucky to be there, and that my father had made it happen.

Joe Erickson never really understood my fascination with cowboy life or my desire to own ranch land. That was a germ I had caught from Mother's side of the family, the Underhills,

Shermans, and Currys, who were pioneer ranchers on the South Plains near Lubbock. Mother raised me on stories of cowboys and ranchers in my family and couldn't have been shocked that the acorn had fallen so close to the tree.

But Mother had died in 1977, leaving me with a father who didn't have a cowboy bone in his body.

It could have been messy. He could have leveled a finger at me and said, "Listen, buster, you're thirty-seven years old and have a wife and two small children. You have no health insurance, no life insurance, no property, no savings, no retirement, no nothing.

"You've gotten yourself wrapped up in two professions that are leading to a dead end. It would be bad enough to have one bad habit, either cowboying or writing, but you've got both. Maybe it's time for you to grow up."

That was exactly the kind of shattering lecture my old man could serve up—truth delivered like a bucket of cold water on a winter day, with a blue-eyed Scandinavian glare that frosted every window in the house. In giving advice to his offspring, he could be fearless and brutal. In later years, when I started my publishing business, I had to sit through many of those sessions.

But in 1980, he chose to wave his magic wand and skipped the lecture.

He didn't understand my cowboy side and I'm not sure he understood the writer side either. Writing was not something that anyone in my family, on either side, had ever done or had even thought about doing. They were all literate people who were steeped in the King James Bible, spoke grammatical English, and wrote good letters, but writing as a profession was nothing an Erickson or a Curry had ever considered.

Back in 1970, I had showed him some of my short stories, but instead of giving me the praise I thought I deserved, he eviscerated me with two words: "So what?" I was furious and didn't show him another piece of writing for years. That didn't bother him, and he didn't ask to read anything else.

Looking back, I know that he was right about those stories. They were rubbish, exactly the kind of hopeless, depressing existential postmodern flapdoodle that was being praised in literary circles and college English departments. Joe was a wise man and an independent thinker, and he asked the right question: "So what?" Two words of truth pried out of hard rock.

In thoughtful moments, he must have wondered, "What is going to become of this kid?" In his place, I would have wondered too—wondered and worried and prayed for some kind of miracle that would lead John into a steady job and some kind of respectable profession that a dad could explain to his friends.

Oh yes, his friends wondered. "What is John doing these days?"

In a small town, everybody is watching. We watch the kids grow up. We watch them go off to college or learn a trade or join the family business. We attend their weddings and know when the babies come. We hear that they've gotten jobs and bought a nice house in Richardson or Plano. If they're injured in a car wreck, get divorced or fired from a job, we know about that too, and it doesn't take long for the news to get around.

My father's circle of friends had watched John march off to UT, walk away from a master's degree at Harvard Divinity School, move back home, work as a farm hand and flunky-bartender at the country club, move off to Oklahoma to punch cows, and now he was doing *what*? Writing books?

Most of what I was doing in those days was invisible to everyone but Kris, but my journal entries reveal that I was putting my early morning writing hours to good use. I had finished several novels and a cowboy memoir called *Cowboy County* and was trying to cultivate a working relationship with two New York agents, Joe Elder and Alex Kamaroff.

I was writing articles for *Western Horseman*, *Livestock Weekly*, and *The Cattleman*, and carrying on a correspondence with editors and writer-friends. My mood veered from high optimism to a dark sense of failure.

I wasn't just sitting around, but my poor father didn't have much encouraging news to pass along to his friends, whose children were doing all the things middle-class people were supposed to be doing in their thirties.

So how did he cope with all this and resist the temptation to roar his disapproval? I ascribe it to three factors. First, he felt an inner assurance that things would turn out all right for me. He respected the man I had become and trusted my decisions, even when he didn't understand them. Also, he knew that I had married an incredibly good woman and that if I messed up everything else, Kris would keep me from going completely off the rails.

Second, he drew peace from his Christian faith and from his deeply held belief that God was at work in people's lives. During my college years, when he had talked about this, I had hardly been able to hide my scorn. "*You think God Almighty cares what happens to people in Perryton, Texas?*"

Yes, that's exactly what he thought, and he didn't flinch or avert his eyes when he said it. "Not even a sparrow falls without God's knowledge," he would say, giving his own paraphrase of Luke 12:7.

Third, Joe was holding a few aces in his hand. He had built up a nice little insurance and real estate business in Perryton. He knew I had no interest in joining him on Main Street but must have suspected that at some point, after I had bloodied my nose enough times running into brick walls, it might be more appealing.

He was right about that. By 1982, I was so tired of failure, so beaten up and frustrated, I was almost ready to join the family business and throw away my silly dreams of being an author.

But before that happened, Hank the Cowdog walked into my life.

CHAPTER 25

MORE THAN A HORSE STORY

"But ask now the beasts, and they shall teach thee, and the fowls of the air, and they shall tell thee."

—Job 12:7–8

The marketplace is a cruel master, and most of the authors I have known went through long periods of lonely rejection. Even Louis L'Amour experienced dark times:

> The early years were harder than anyone can imagine. . . . It is never easy to be hungry, never easy to be alone, never easy to believe in oneself when nobody else does. . . . Reading through the old journals, one begins to read between the lines and sense the doubt, the hope, the fear of what lies ahead (L'Amour 1990, 168).

By 1981 I had written four novels that were sitting in boxes. I was sending query letters and sample chapters to publishing companies whose names and addresses I found in *Writer's Market*. Most of my query letters brought anonymous rejection slips and I had collected hundreds of them, maybe a thousand.

A few of the query letters drew a personal response from editors who took the time to write encouraging notes with their rejection slips. Lew Howland, an editor at Little, Brown and Company in Boston, turned down all four of my novels but always did it in a pleasant way: "This is an interesting story idea and you have good writing skills, but it misses the mark in subtle ways." I appreciated his personal comments but never figured out what to do about a novel that "missed the mark in subtle ways."

Another rejection letter is worth mentioning. It came from an editor I met at a WWA convention. She represented a major New York publishing house and was one of those editors a young nobody-writer like me needed to cultivate, so I tried.

She seemed as different from me as a Martian. She was East Coast down to the marrow of her bones and knew nothing about the frontier culture that had produced me and about which I was writing. How she had ended up as an editor of Western novels, I couldn't imagine. It must have been a temporary assignment that she hoped would lead to something better.

In person, she struck me as a woman without much character. My mother would have described her as "cheap," but she held a master's degree in literature from some fine college in New England and had retained a gloss of sophistication. She had chosen to be who she was, and she had the power to make or break aspiring writers.

I talked to her about ideas for several Western novels and she showed interest in stories that involved a character based on my

Grandmother Curry. She suggested that I write up a sample chapter and summary and submit them. If she liked them, she would go to the editorial board and push for approval. Maybe we could do some business.

In those days, "maybe" was almost as exciting as "yes." Back home at the ranch, I plunged into the task and spent my writing hours typing up my best effort at a novel summary, sent it off in a nice package, first-class mail, and waited. Weeks passed and at last the letter came, written on the firm's official stationery. It contained several paragraphs and concluded with this bizarre sentence: "This novel has too much integrity and not enough sex."

Years later, I was able to see the humor in that, but at the time it left me close to despair. What do you do when your writing has too much integrity? I howled like a wounded beast.

But life went on. I was getting poor marks in the novel business but kept writing short humorous pieces about my experiences as a cowboy. I knew I could get them published in livestock journals and had even found some success with the *Dallas Morning News*, *Dallas Times Herald*, *Fort Worth Star-Telegram*, and *Texas Highways*.

In January 1981, while I was working on the LZ Ranch, I called Dale Seagraves, who had replaced Paul Horn as editor of *The Cattleman*, and asked if he would buy a series of twelve humorous articles (a year's supply) about cowboy life. He was interested and offered to pay $100 apiece. I said I wanted $150. He thought it over, called me back, and said he would take twelve articles at $150 each.

I went to work on the series the very next morning and, over a three-week period, cranked out fourteen articles. (Two of them were published in *Western Horseman*.) I wrote them as fast as I could, giving no thought to style, structure, voicing, point of view, or other matters that might concern an author of "literature."

I didn't think of them as literature. I was just writing about subjects I knew very well, dashing them off as fast as I could, and looking forward to receiving a paycheck. In a journal entry, I said only, "They are good."

CASEY THE BRONC

The first six articles dealt with specific experiences I'd had working on the ranch—roping episodes, counting cattle, and doctoring sick yearlings. They were humorous nonfiction articles.

But then I wrote a story about a horse-breaking adventure Tom Ellzey and I had recently gone through with a five-year-old bay gelding named Casey, but instead of writing it from *my* point of view, I let Casey tell it in his own voice: "Diary of a Bronc."

Something happened when I wrote that story, and today, more than forty years later, I see it as a watershed event in my writing career. For one thing, it was my first attempt at telling a story from the point of view of an animal, a technique I later applied in the Hank the Cowdog books.

But it was more than an experiment in voicing. "Diary of a Bronc" had depth and substance that didn't originate in the *head* or come from some book of literary criticism. It had levels of meaning that resonated beyond the pages of type.

On one level, it was an honest, carefully observed description of a horse-breaking experience. In their natural state, horses are lazy, willful, and brutal. They despise all forms of training and discipline. They resist the work that might dignify their lives. Left to themselves, they would do nothing but fight, breed, and eat. Without the discipline imposed by human masters, they would *not* be noble and free. They would be something close to worthless.

On a deeper level, the story sounded almost biblical—a parable of sin, pride, and disobedience—but it wasn't preachy. It was funny. Today, I scratch my head and wonder, "Where did that come from?" By 1981, Kris and I were attending church and singing in the Methodist church choir, but I wasn't reading books by Christian authors or studying the Bible or trying to write stories with a message.

I can only guess that in a quiet moment, when I wasn't stalking a literary style or trying to be profound, I reached into the closet of my subconscious mind and pulled out an old suit of clothes that had been hanging there, unused, for many years. When I tried it on, it fit.

It was a radical departure from the fiction that was being published in upscale magazines and literary journals of the time and from the literary styles I had encountered in college. "Diary of a Bronc" dealt with the experience of two cowboys trying to break and train a horse, but it didn't treat ordinary experience or ordinary people as absurd. The characters had dignity, the work had meaning, and the chords of the story found resolution.

During my writing apprenticeship, I had tried on dozens of literary costumes and they hadn't fit me, but this one did. The device of telling a story through the eyes and voice of Casey the Bronc established a template for stories that could escape the dark conclusions of secular realism.

The Devil in Texas has been out of print for several decades, which means that many readers have never encountered "Diary of a Bronc." I have a solution for that. Read on.*

* In 2024, Maverick Books reissued this collection of stories under the new title *Confessions of a Cowdog and Other Cowboy Stories.* The change called attention to the book's most notable feature, that it contains the first-ever appearance of Hank the Cowdog.

CHAPTER 26

CASEY THE BRONC

• • •

"Diary of a Bronc"*

MAY 1

Casey's my name, being an outlaw's my game. I'm five years old and never been rode. First man that tries me is gonna get throwed.

My momma ate dynamite and washed it down with gasoline. My old man ate pitchforks and rattlesnakes and barbed wire. He never walked around a tree. He'd just kick it down and stomp on it.

* Originally published in *Western Horseman*, February 1982. Reprinted in *The Devil in Texas and Other Cowboy Tales* (Maverick Books, 1982).

I'm a bad dude, fellers, so give me some room. The world owes me a living and I intend to collect. If I kill a couple of men along the way, it'll just be icing on my cake.

I want to hit the rodeo circuit, see. That's the place for this boy: show business, the easy life, work eight seconds a week, man, throw some little snuff-dipping cowboy through the fence, then eat prairie hay the rest of the time.

But hey, baby, I'm stuck out here on a nickel and dime cattle ranch in Texas. Ain't no bright lights around here. Ain't no excitement. The company's dull. My public's waiting for me up in Cheyenne.

I've got to get out of this place.

MAY 4

Man, these horses I have to live with around here are OLD and TIRED and CORNY. Like their idea of excitement is biting each other at the hay feeder. Ain't that wild? Ain't that western?

What a bunch of scrubs.

Yesterday, old fat-boy Happy took a bite out of the Shetland pony and ran him around the corral. Thought he was pretty tough. I said, "Say, Hoss, try that little action on me."

Heh. He tried. If he hadn't weighed twelve hundred pounds, I'd have kicked him clean through the calf shed. Then that little Cookie mare came along, had her ears pinned down, trying to look mean. I cleaned house on her and said, "Okay, who's next?"

That's when old Popeye came up. He's, ahem, *the elder statesman* of the horse pasture. He'll weigh thirteen hundred, but he don't fight. Like, he's above that childish stuff. He's ate up with religion.

He said, "Casey, you're causing a lot of trouble around here."

And I said, "You got that right, Pops, only I ain't really got cranked up yet. When I do, y'all better hunt a hole."

"One of these days you're going to come to grief."

"You gonna do it?"

"I might play a part in it."

Man, I laughed in his face. "You handle the preachin', Pops, and I'll take care of the outlaw stuff, okay?"

The old fool just walked off. What could he say?

MAY 5

Life's getting exciting. The cowboys think it's time I was broke to a saddle. This morning they tried to catch me. That was a scream. Like, they tried to slip up and put a halter on me, talking that "whoa-boy-easy-bronc" stuff.

They got me in a corner, see, and thought they had me licked. Heh. I took the top two boards out of the corral fence and went on my way. Next time, I'll flatten the whole corral. And stomp on it.

MAY 6

They got a rope halter on me. Ran me into a chute before I could really get my destructive trip going. Ah, who cares? A halter don't mean nuthin' to me. I'll just break it.

MAY 7

Didn't I say I'd break that halter? They tied me to a post, see, and I just went back on the rope and . . . bingo! No more halter. Kind of wish it hadn't broke. Had my heart set on jerking that post out of the ground.

MAY 8

These cowboys don't give up. They put a heavy nylon halter on me and they've got some kind of new rig on the snubbing post. They tied an inner tube to the post and they're fixing to tie ME to the inner tube.

That's cool. I'd just as soon tear up an inner tube as anything else.

LATER

Inner tubes don't tear up so easy. I fought that thing for an hour and a half, and I'm so tired I can hardly move. That's okay, it's all going according to my plan. Tomorrow I'm gonna give 'em TOTAL DESTRUCTION—post, inner tube, ropes, halter, corrals, barns, the whole son of a gun.

When I get done, man, we gonna have a big pile of TOOTHPICKS around here.

MAY 9

I ain't ever been treated like this before. They stuck me on that inner tube and sacked me out 'til the world looked level. High Loper had a saddle blanket and Slim used his vest, and fellers, they worked me over. I gave it my best shot, but I got a feeling that I lost.

Okay, I've played around long enough. Tomorrow—total, absolute, utter DESTRUCTION! Cowboys too.

MAY 10

Maybe tomorrow.

MAY 11

I've got a funny feeling about this deal. That inner tube has wore me plumb out. The harder I pull back on it, the harder it slings me into the post. It could be a losing proposition.

MAY 12

Ha! They throwed a saddle on Preacher Popeye and clipped a

lead rope onto my halter. They think Popeye's going to take me out into the pasture for a little stroll.

Well, hey, I've got news for them. They beat me on the inner tube, but when they put me one-on-one against another horse, man, we gonna have some violence and bloodshed. I've got a few tricks saved up for Popeye.

LATER

Pops is stouter than you might think.

LATER

I guess you might say that I'm halter broke. Slim snubbed me up to Popeye. I went back on the rope and fought like a wildcat, figured I could jerk Pops off his feet.

Pops jerked *me* off *my* feet, out of my tracks, almost out of my skin, and hauled me around the pasture like I was nothing but a smoked ham on a piece of string.

I fought him for a hundred yards, man, and decided that religion didn't hurt him none in the Stouts Department. I've got whiplash all the way from my nose to the tip of my tail. May have to change my stragedy.

MAY 13

Say, baby, what is this? Did I hear High Loper say that he's gonna climb on my back today? No way is that dude gonna climb on my back, 'cause my momma ate dynamite and washed it down with . . .

LATER

He done it.

MAY 14

He done it again. These guys don't play fair. They won't fight me when I'm fresh and full of vinegar. They put me on that inner tube and then they hook me up to Pops and let him drag me around the pasture 'til I'm tired. By the time they start climbing into the saddle, I'm bushed, man, wore out. It ain't fair.

MAY 15

I'm beat. I surrender. They're winning.

MAY 16

Actually . . . it ain't so bad. Today I learned a little bit about neck reining. I've learned how to stop and go, and back up on command. I hate to admit it, but . . . well, I'm kind of proud of myself.

MAY 17

Loper and I made our first solo trip out into the pasture. I did a good job, I tried hard. I think Loper was proud of me.

MAY 20

We worked cattle today for the first time. Know what? I'm good at this, I really am, and durned if I don't kind of enjoy it.

JUNE 2

I went to my first roundup today. I wasn't the star of the show, but I held my territory and did my job. I've noticed that the other horses are nicer to me now. They treat me with . . . respect.

JULY 15

I guess I'll never make it to the Cheyenne rodeo, but I've sort of lost my desire for the high life. I've got a good job here, friends, a nice place to live. Maybe that's enough.

AUGUST 15

We've got a new colt in the herd, name's Chief, thinks he's hot stuff, says they're never going to break *him* to ride.

I had a little talk with him. I said, "See that big bay horse over there? His name's Popeye and he's *mucho caballo.* When the time comes, he'll make a Christian out of you."

The kid laughed in my face, called me an old duffer. These dadgum kids. They've got no respect for their elders. You can't tell 'em anything.

I think this younger generation is going to Hell in a bucket!

• • •

I had so much fun with Casey the Bronc, the next morning I wrote "Log of a Cow Horse," a story that was narrated by another horse on the LZ Ranch. And the next morning, without a moment of thought, I dashed off a story narrated by a ranch dog named Hank, "Confessions of a Cowdog." I wrote it in one three-hour writing session, turned out the light, left my office, and went to work on the LZ Ranch.

On February 1, 1981, I made an entry in my journal. "This is Sunday, a day of reflection. I spent the week writing more humor articles. My pace slowed and I only got three good ones written: 'Log of a Cowhorse,' 'Confessions of a Cowdog,' and 'The World's First Cowboy.'"

There was nothing in this entry to suggest that I considered "Confessions of a Cowdog" any better than the other two stories I had written that week. The character of Hank didn't come as an epiphany or with a display of fireworks, and I never dreamed that he would become a star. I was writing for money, not for literature, fame, or posterity.

FROM NONFICTION TO FICTION

The first Hank story crossed the line between a nonfiction article and a fictional short story, in effect creating a new literary form. This occurred in such a quiet manner that even the editor didn't notice, or didn't object. That is surprising because magazine editors have strict rules about what they will and won't publish. *The Cattleman* published *no fiction* and made that very clear in their guidelines for writers.

The Cattleman audience (cowboys and ranchers, predominantly male) didn't read fiction, except maybe the novels of Louis L'Amour and Elmer Kelton. They didn't trust the genre and considered "fiction" another word for a lie or distortion of the truth. If you had conducted a poll of *Cattleman* subscribers and asked if they read short stories, they would have said **no**, absolutely not. The short story form belonged to English professors and literary types, the same crowd that was drawn to jazz and abstract art.

That first Hank short story *was* a work of fiction, but it blurred the hard line between imagination and reality. It operated in an environment of hard fact and observation (I knew the details of ranch life to the bone), but the story was narrated by a dog, which made it pure fiction. It slipped past the editor, ran in the magazine, and those old ranchers never uttered a peep.

The story allowed sunlight and humor to brighten a work of fiction, and it was handcrafted for the people in my own region and hometown.

CHAPTER 27

DEAD END

In July 1981, after our spring branding, I left the LZ Ranch and took a job as a carpenter's helper. My boss was Clarence Parrish, a skilled, meticulous carpenter who specialized in finish work—countertops, cabinets, and trim, the things you see when you walk into a house.

Framing carpenters can hide their mistakes behind drywall and plaster, but the work of a finish carpenter is there for everyone to see, and it had better be perfect. With Clarence, it always was.

He had gotten a contract to build a house out in the country south of Perryton, and though he had the temperament of a man who preferred to work alone, he hired two hands to help him: me and Jeff Knighton. Jeff was engaged to Clarence's daughter Linda and would later become his son-in-law.

Jeff had grown up in Perryton, so we had a long history in common. Our parents were friends, and his father was the assistant director of the high school band, of which I was a member (bassoon). When Mr. Knighton needed a drummer for the stage band, he recruited me and taught me how to play the drums.

Like me, Jeff had gone off to college, then moved back to Perryton. He was in a period of transition, unsure of what he wanted to do with his life, and had taken the construction job to help Clarence and to give himself time to think about the future. (He ended up going to seminary and became a United Church of Christ minister with an earned doctorate.)

While we worked at the construction site, Jeff and I had opportunities to talk about a wide range of topics: current events, local news, literature, music, and theology, as well as our personal hopes, dreams, and problems. There weren't many local people I could talk to about my secret life as a writer, but Jeff was sympathetic and interested, so I told him about my aspirations and frustrations.

In the fall of 1981, I was feeling optimistic about my future and thought that I was close to making a breakthrough. (Foolish dreamer.) Three of my nonfiction books had been published, so I was no longer suffering in total obscurity.* When I told people that I was a writer, I could say it without blushing.

The Cattleman had accepted the twelve-part series of articles I mentioned above and another twelve-part series I had written on the history and evolution of roping technique. I had gotten several articles published in the Sunday magazine of the *Dallas Morning News*, which seemed a big deal at the time. I had applied for a Guggenheim Fellowship and had sent the outline for a series of Western novels to Irwyn Applebaum at Bantam Books.

* *Through Time and the Valley* (Shoal Creek Publishers, 1978); *Panhandle Cowboy* (University of Nebraska Press, 1980); *The Modern Cowboy* (University of Nebraska Press, 1981).

I was particularly excited about the contact with Bantam. At WWA conventions, I had gotten acquainted with Irwyn and had learned that Bantam wanted to develop several young writers to strengthen its line of Western novels. Louis L'Amour had been their bread and butter for decades, but he was in his eighties and slowing down. I hoped that I might become a Bantam author.

Every afternoon when I returned home from work, I rushed to the mail to see if I'd gotten a reply from the Guggenheim Foundation or Bantam. December came and went, then January and February. Jeff and I were working outside in the snow and I told him, "This would be a great time for me to get some good news from New York."

GREAT DARKNESS

The two replies arrived in March, and both began, "We regret to inform you . . ." I had gone through years of disappointment and should have been hardened against the pain of a rejection letter. I tried to hide my disappointment from Kris, but inside, I was crushed. In my journal, I wrote, "We are alone in our struggle for survival. My highest hopes have been dashed on the rocks."

I went to my writing office the next morning at 4:30 and tried to maintain my normal routine. I returned to the house at 7:15 and waited for Jeff to pick me up, but I didn't feel right—light in the head, abstract, unreal. My hands and feet felt cold. I grew weak in the knees and thought I was going to black out.

I sat down and waited for the sensation to pass. When Jeff arrived at 7:30, I told him to go on without me. I was sick and needed to stay in bed. I didn't mention the rejection slips, but maybe he figured it out.

I spent an entire day and the following night in bed, tormented by dreams of death and failure, grieving over a sorrow that was too great to express, even to Kris. Never in my life had I thought I would end up a failure, but that was the abyss that had opened up in front of me.

My sleep that night was haunted by terrible dreams. I was a wounded deer, being stalked by wolves. For years, I had escaped them, but now I was exhausted and leaving a blood trail, and they were closing in for the kill. I am reminded of that dark time every time I read Psalm 22: "*I am poured out like water, and all my bones are out of joint: my heart is like wax; it is melted in the midst of my bowels. My strength is dried up like a potsherd and my tongue cleaveth to my jaws; and thou hast brought me into the dust of death*" (Psalms 22:14–15]).

For twenty-four hours, I thought I was going to die. But I didn't.

The next morning, Jeff picked me up at the usual time and I told him about my ordeal. I wasn't going to roll over and die. If I couldn't get my books published in the conventional way, I would have to do something else.

People in my region needed good stories, and I had spent the last fifteen years learning how to write them. I didn't need the permission of editors or publishers or agents or critics. All I needed was *readers*, and I thought I could find them right where I lived.

I was going to start my own publishing company—in Perryton, in my garage. I had already thought of a name for the business: Maverick Books. In Texas history, "maverick" was the name old-time cowpunchers gave to cattle that lived in the wild and carried no brand. It seemed appropriate.

As Jeff and I worked in the cold, I raved on for hours and he listened to all of it. Then he smiled and laid a hand on my shoulder. "Good for you."

CHAPTER 28

VILLAGE HANDYMAN

At the end of March 1982, Clarence, Jeff, and I finished the framing, roofing, and drywall at the construction site, and what remained was the kind of inside finish work that Clarence had made into a specialty. He really didn't need me anymore, so I went into business for myself as a village handyman.

I wasn't skilled enough to do the kind of carpentry work Clarence did, but I had learned about framing, roofing, tape-and-bed work, simple electrical wiring, and basic plumbing, and thought I could make a living doing small jobs that the real craftsmen in town didn't want.

I started doing repairs on some of my father's rental houses. By the time I finished those jobs, he put out the word to his circle of friends that if they had problems that needed simple repairs, I was in that business. I charged fifteen dollars an hour (twice what I'd been making before) and did no advertising, and never missed a day of work.

What I discovered was that in a small town, you can make a good living as a handyman, and nobody cares what you *don't* know. What matters is that you tell the truth, show up on time, and provide honest service. If a job was too big for my skills, I didn't take it. If the customer hadn't been satisfied with my work, I wouldn't have charged for my time.

I was on my own in this business and couldn't run to Clarence if I got in over my head, and it was scary at first. I bought a Time-Life series of twenty books on home repairs and every morning before I went to the job site, I read the sections that explained the kind of work I would be doing. I didn't take the books with me to the job, figuring it wouldn't inspire confidence in my customers.

I followed this pattern for five months, made more money than I'd ever dreamed possible, and left my customers grateful for the good work.

In July, I did some handyman jobs for a local realtor, John Beasley, who owned several houses that needed small repairs: doors that didn't close, cracks in the walls, water-stained ceilings, and light switches that didn't work. He was pleased with my work, and I got along well with him. He paid on time, his checks were good, and he left me alone on the job.

One day he hit me up with a proposal. A local man had come to him and said, "Why don't you buy my rental house? I'm sick of it." John suggested that we partner on the house. I could fix it up and he would handle the sales end of the deal. "I think we can get it at a bargain price and make some money."

It appeared to be an ideal fixer-upper house, structurally sound but neglected. The yard hadn't been mowed or watered in months, and the paint on the outside was faded and peeling.

Several faucets leaked, the inside walls needed a coat of bright paint, and the carpet looked awful—old, worn, dirty, and peppered with deposits of petrified cat manure.

We decided to buy the house and John made it easy. He had a line of credit at the bank, we both signed the note, and he took care of all the paperwork. For the next two months, that's where I worked. I mowed the yard, hauled off weeds and junk, and turned on some sprinklers to revive the lawn.

I gave the house a thorough cleaning, tore out all the carpet and replaced it with good used carpet, gave the walls a fresh coat of paint, and replaced all the faucets, light switches, and electrical plugs.

This house was located only three blocks from our home on Baylor Street. I bought a little stock tank, put it in the backyard, and filled it with water. On hot afternoons, our two children, Scot and Ashley, walked over to the job site and played in their own private swimming pool.

I worked hard on the house and enjoyed every minute of it. Not only was it satisfying to restore a dirty, neglected little hovel and make it into something better, but I loved being independent and working for myself. I had never responded well to being watched by a boss.

I've been told that this independent spirit is a characteristic of Scots-Irish people. In the old country, they never got along with landlords, bosses, bishops, priests, squires, or kings, and that was the main reason they came to America. They wanted to work for themselves and to be left alone.

I got a strong dose of Scotch-Irish genes from both sides of my family, the Curry-Shermans on Mother's side and the Hustons on Joe's side.

I finished the house in August, and it looked nice. The man who had sold it to us had seen only the flaws, but with new carpet, fresh paint, and a thorough cleaning, it looked like a different house. Beasley put it on the market and sold it within days. Each of us walked away with a profit of twenty-five hundred dollars.

That and a bank loan became my grubstake for Maverick Books.

JERRY

One of the nice things about being in business for myself was that I could set my own hours. That came in handy toward the end of June, because I wanted to attend the Western Writers of America convention in Santa Fe.

I had developed a friendship with a young novelist named Jerry O'Brien (not his real name), and it happened that he would be driving to the convention and passing through the Panhandle. We decided that he should stop in Perryton for a few days and we would drive together to Santa Fe.

I had met Jerry in 1980 at the WWA gathering in Boulder, where he had been the golden boy of the convention: young, blond-headed, clear-eyed, handsome, modest, dedicated to his craft, and quite successful. At convention gatherings, he always drew a crowd of editors and agents.

Although only in his thirties, he had become a full-time professional writer and was making a good living for his wife and children. The contrast between me and Jerry could hardly have been sharper. He had figured out how to deal with New York editors and a major paperback house had published several of his novels.

At the Santa Fe convention, he planned to meet with his editor and discuss a project that would involve a series of three novels. It was a big deal. Jerry was moving up.

I, on the other hand, had done so poorly with editors and agents that I was planning to publish my own work. In most book crowds, self-publishing was regarded as a kiss of death, certainly nothing to brag about. If you had to publish your own books, it meant that everybody who knew anything about the book business had turned you down.

In our correspondence, I had told Jerry about my plans for Maverick Books, and he applauded the idea. He said it was a sensible, courageous course of action.

I made the trip to Santa Fe, lying down in the back of Jerry's van. Several days earlier, I had helped Jeff Knighton roof a house that had been damaged in a hailstorm. While ripping out the old shingles, I injured my back and had to leave the job. Roofing was the hardest, most unpleasant work I'd ever tried, and I sincerely hoped that I would never have to do it again. My experience as a roofer gave me a powerful incentive to make my book business a success.

SANTA FE

Jerry and I rolled into Santa Fe around five o'clock in the evening and checked into our hotel. Jerry could have taken a room by himself (he had the means), but to help me save some money, he suggested that we share a room.

We showered and cleaned up and made our way to the convention hotel, the Loretta. On the fourth floor, we found the WWA contingent making merry in the "hospitality room," a sanitized name for the bar. At writers' conventions, it was always a busy place.

Later, we went to a restaurant with a group of old veteran writers who had been working under contract with major paperback publishers in New York, often under pseudonyms. One of them said that he "cranked out" a book every month and another claimed to have published a hundred novels.

After downing several drinks, one of them leaned across the

table and growled, "Like everyone else at this table, I'm a hack." I took that to mean that he wrote the kind of novels he wouldn't want his mother to read—"adult Westerns," they were called.

Walking back to the hotel, Jerry and I talked about that. Everybody else at the table might have considered himself a hack, but we didn't.

The next day, I attended some panel discussions and visited with old friends (Don Worcester, Judy Alter, Elmer Kelton, Jeanne Williams, Don Coldsmith). I even spoke with some New York editors. Jerry had encouraged me to keep talking to them, as he thought there still might be a chance that I could get something published with a major house.

"Make the editors feel important," he told me. "Let them suggest changes to your book and feel that they're part of the process. That way, they'll push hard for your book in editorial meetings. They all have fragile egos. Ask for their advice and sign the contract, then write [your book] the way you want it. But *get the contract*."

I had a long conversation with Irwyn Applebaum and to my surprise, he expressed an interest in getting the mass market paperback rights to two of my nonfiction books, *Panhandle Cowboy* and *The Modern Cowboy*, both of which had been published by the University of Nebraska Press. He had read them and passed them around to other people at Bantam, and everyone agreed they were solid books. He even encouraged me to submit some outlines for novels. If I came up with something he liked, he would submit it to the editorial board.

That conversation raised my hopes again, but nothing ever came of it. At conventions, everyone can talk and make big plans. When the convention is over, the hotel employees sweep the floor and turn out the lights, and everybody goes back to the things they were doing before. Or so it always was with me.

While I was busy at the convention, Jerry had his big meeting with the editor. He had brought a finished manuscript of a novel and outlines for two more, a three-book series. In the afternoon, I looked for him in the convention hotel. He had expected the meeting to go well and I was anxious to hear the good news.

When I returned to our hotel room around six, he was sitting in a chair and his face was ashen. He tried to put on a cheerful front, but he was devastated. His editor had told him the finished novel was unacceptable, and he didn't like the outlines either. The fellow was sorry, but he couldn't offer a contract.

Jerry and his wife had just moved into a new house and were counting on the advance money to make their payments. Now, they would have to put the house on the market and he didn't know what he would do—sell cars or maybe get into real estate.

One meeting with an editor had turned his life upside down.

We didn't go back to the convention but ate by ourselves in a little Mexican restaurant near our hotel. I tried to offer encouragement, but there wasn't much I could say. The irony was painful. We had started the trip with Jerry trying to cheer *me* up, and now I was trying to comfort him. All at once, self-publishing didn't appear to be such a bad option.

That experience made a lasting impression on me. In the writing business, you never have it made, no matter how successful you think you are, because a small group of people in a distant city are making decisions that determine your future.

I promised myself that I would never put my fate in the hands of an editor in New York.

CHAPTER 29

MAVERICK BOOKS

I have often wondered where I ever got the idea that someone living in a small Texas town could publish his own books. I think my model might have come from cowboy cartoonist Ace Reid. Back in the seventies, when I was working on cowboy crews along the Beaver River, Ace Reid's name often came up in conversations as we were driving herds of slow-moving cattle across big pastures.

Usually, one of the cowboys had seen a *Cowpokes* cartoon in the local paper that described a funny incident from his own experience, or one of the men described a cow at the drag-end of the herd as "an Ace Reid special." Everyone knew what that meant: a thin parody of a healthy animal, probably with an evil disposition.

Those references to Ace Reid came up on a regular basis among these men, who had his cartoons taped to refrigerator doors and kept their work schedules scribbled on a *Cowpokes* calendar that hung on the wall beside the telephone.

To me, Ace was a legend, and I didn't even know if he was still alive, but on one occasion, the man who brought up Ace's name knew something about the artist. Ace lived on a small ranch outside of Kerrville, Texas, and he self-published and distributed his own books, syndicated cartoons, and calendars.

Self-publishing. That was an interesting idea. I had spent years sending off query letters to publishers and harvesting a big crop of rejection slips, but old Ace had published his own work. Hmmm.

When I decided to start Maverick Books, I can't say that I was thinking about Ace or making a conscious attempt to follow his lead, yet I'm sure it was in the back of my mind. Sometimes the most important information we can possess about a bold venture is that it's not impossible. I must have carried the thought, "If Ace did it, maybe I can too."

BAXTER BLACK

I didn't know it at the time, but an author in Colorado was having the same thoughts and, like me, he used Ace Reid as a model. His name was Baxter Black, a large-animal veterinarian who had come up with a perfectly outrageous idea: to become a poet for folks in the Heartland who operated feedlots and dairies, raised corn and soybeans, and ran cattle.

Had he done a bit of market research, he would have known that the demographic he wanted to reach, farmers and ranchers, seldom went to bookstores and didn't purchase many books. When they did, it wasn't poetry.

Had he spent more time in college literature classes, he would have known that poetry was a fossil medium, driven into extinction by practitioners who had proved that if you remove meter, rhyme, and joy from a poem, you have nothing left but a melancholy husk—and nobody will read it, much less pay for it.

Had Baxter asked my opinion, I would have given the obvious answer: poetry in the United States was as dead as a skunk in the middle of a busy highway. But he didn't ask me or any other sensible person for advice.

Instead, he followed the lead of old Ace Reid, bypassed the arbiters of literary fashion, found an ag journalist who would back him (Harry Green in Denver), published his own poetry books, and went directly to an audience of readers that nobody dreamed was there—an audience that wasn't there until he created it from scratch.

He wrote precision-built verses that resurrected the ancient qualities of the poetic form (rhyme and meter) and gave them fresh life by adding humor.

Rhythm and rhyme are elements of natural beauty that are accessible to anyone, but most of us occupy a world that is out of rhythm and doesn't rhyme. When we read Baxter's poetry, we are suddenly confronted by flashes of beauty that come from a rearrangement of the language we speak every day. We recognize the words, but Baxter gives them an order we never dreamed was there.

I have noticed a similar effect in pastures after a spring rain. One day the land is drab and winter-dead, and the next, it explodes into acres of wildflowers: colors, patterns, and geometry that cause us to gasp in wonder and delight.

I didn't get acquainted with Baxter until 1983, when he and his wife Cindy Lou were on their way to an appearance in Guymon, Oklahoma. He called me on the phone and asked if they could come by our house for a visit. By that time, he had published several books and so had I, and we were both doing literary tricks on the high trapeze, with no net to catch us if we fell.

I have always been amazed by the uncanny similarities between my career path and Baxter's: gentle humor, self-publishing, performing our work to live audiences, and scratching out a living in places where conventional booksellers seldom left a track. It's as though we had read the same book or attended the same graduate school or used the same consulting firm, but that's not the way it happened.

What we had in common was cowboy stubbornness, an entrepreneurial spirit, a love for small towns and country people, and admiration for the accomplishments of Ace Reid. To that, we added natural, homegrown talent, and Baxter had plenty of it. We would have to measure his talent by the acre, not by the square inch.

THE FIRST BOOK

I decided that my first Maverick book would be the collection of humor articles I had done for *Western Horseman* and *The Cattleman*, including some of my favorite stories: "The World's First Cowboy," "Diary of a Bronc," and "Sally May's Journal." Those stories were funny. I had read them aloud to small groups in Perryton and they had gone over well.

Gerald Holmes had done pen and ink illustrations for those stories when they ran in the magazines, so that part was already done. Gerald and his wife Carol lived out in the country north of Perryton and he worked for a local feedlot. Back in 1976, we had met at the country home of a mutual friend, cowboy photographer Bill Ellzey.

Gerald showed me some of his drawings and I liked them at once. He seemed to be doing with pictures the sort of thing I wanted to do with words: describing ranch life in a manner that was honest, funny, and aesthetically pleasing.

From the start, I never gave Gerald any advice or instructions about his illustrations, and he was the one who put faces on all the characters in the Hank the Cowdog stories. My approach with him was the same as I have used with other people who have worked with me over the years: identify the best people, tell them what you want, and leave them alone. I have found that to be a good policy.*

We needed a logo for Maverick Books, so I turned to the same gifted lady who had always risen to a challenge: my wife Kris. Though she had a degree in interior design and could have found a career in the working world, she had always preferred to devote her skills and energy to her home and family. She never wanted to be a professional woman and I was glad. We managed to get along with one salary, though it was never easy.

One of the benefits in this arrangement was that I had a partner working beside me every step of the way, using her talents and intelligence to help me in my professional life.

When we started Maverick Books I needed an editor, and Kris became my editor. When I needed a photographer to illustrate my nonfiction books, she bought a camera and learned how to use it. When I needed a musician to help with my Hank performances, she bought a mandolin and chord book and learned to play. She already knew how to sing and had a beautiful soprano voice, high, sweet, and clear, with a natural vibrato.

Now I needed a logo for Maverick Books. She bought ink, pens, and drafting paper and tools, and spent a week working on the dining table. She had never designed a logo, but it never occurred to her that she *couldn't*. She didn't get paid and was pregnant with our son Mark but never murmured a word of complaint. She came up with a great design and we still use it today, more than forty years later.

* Gerald illustrated more than eighty books for me and died in 2019 after a long illness. We never quarreled and he never missed a deadline.

Next, I found a typesetter/book designer in Lincoln, Nebraska, Tom Sheahan. I told him my general ideas for the book. I wanted him to design a trade paperback that was attractive (good paper, clear print, good binding, attractive cover), that could be sold at a price people in my community could afford, but also a book we could manufacture cheaply enough so that we could make a profit.

Making a profit was crucial. This wasn't going to be a little artsy-craftsy venture, subsidized by grants from the National Endowment for the Arts or the Small Business Administration. It was a serious business venture, and we had to make money. Self-publishing was going to be my lifeboat in a stormy sea, and we had to do it right.

Over the next several months, Kris and I read proofs and made decisions about the designs Tom Sheahan came up with. In August, he sent the camera-ready material to Cushing Malloy, a printing firm in Ann Arbor, Michigan, and we were on our way.

THE BANKER

At that point, I had one more job to do: talk to a banker and arrange a line of credit so that when I received my first shipment of books, I could pay Tom Sheahan and Cushing Malloy. I calculated that I would need two thousand dollars. Today, that doesn't sound like much money, but to Kris and me, it was a substantial sum. I knew that my father would have loaned me the money, but I preferred not to trouble him.

I set up a meeting with Keith Good, a senior vice president at the First Bank and Trust in Booker, a small town fifteen miles east of Perryton. Keith and I had known each other since grade school, and between 1974 and 1978, I worked for him, managing a ranch for his trust department. He knew everyone in my family and I knew everyone in his.

Keith was aware of my secret life as an author and had always been supportive, and he was pleased when I told him what I had in mind with Maverick Books. He listened to my proposal and said, "We can make that work. We'll fix you up with a line of credit, and if you need more, come see me. Good luck."

Years later, I often thought about that meeting. Keith was a good friend, but he was also a banker who had to answer to stockholders and bank examiners. Any bank examiner who had looked at my loan would have choked. "This guy wants to start a *publishing company* in a town that doesn't even have a bookstore? Keith, not only does this kid have nothing in the way of assets, but you might have heard that the national economy is going through the worst recession since the thirties."

I never asked Keith about this, but I have an idea that when I left the bank, he put in a call to Joseph W. Erickson, my father. "Joe," he might have said, "I just set up your son with a two-thousand-dollar line of credit. He wants to start a publishing company. Strictly speaking, I shouldn't make this loan . . ."

And I would guess that Joe interrupted him: "I'll guarantee the loan." Maybe he went to the bank and co-signed the note or maybe it was just a handshake deal between two men with integrity. Keith understood that if Joe gave his word, that was enough. In those days, bankers could do business that way.

It was the kind of thing that happened every day in small towns. Good people found ways of working around the system so that someone in the community could build a dream, start a business, buy a home . . . reach for the stars. From his office on Main Street, my father helped good people do good things and never told anyone about it.

I know, because years later, after he died, those people came up to me in stores, at the post office, at wedding receptions, after church—and thanked me for his acts of kindness. I told them, "Yes, I know all about his kindness."

Joe had a great deal of confidence in me and my crazy dream of publishing my own books, and he continued providing us with investment capital. By the time he died in 1989, we owed his estate $50,000. Gary Rinker had joined me by then, taking care of accounting and business affairs, and we paid every dollar back to the estate. It took us several years, but we got 'er done.

BILL SHEARER

In the fall of 1982, I was using my early morning hours to prepare for the launch of Maverick Books and came up with an interesting idea: I should try to purchase the rights to my first book, *Through Time and the Valley*. That would give us two books to sell, instead of just one.

Shoal Creek Publishers had brought out the book in hardback in 1978 and it had gone into a second printing, then into a paperback edition. In 1981, Luther Thompson decided to retire and sold Shoal Creek to a young man named Bill Shearer. I had never met him but had heard a good deal about him. He was regarded as a rising star of Texas publishing.

He went to work for Texas A&M University Press right out of college. After a few years of learning the book trade, he and his wife Kathy went out on their own and started Shearer Publishing. They bought an old dance hall/beer garden in Fredericksburg and converted it into a warehouse and office. They found a market niche for maps and tourist guides, and their *Roads of Texas* sold well.

When they purchased Shoal Creek Publishers, they expanded into Texas history and fiction. Bill had a good eye for design and brought out beautiful books. He was also a smart marketer. He had figured out how to get his books reviewed in major newspapers and how to do business with the bookstore chains in Dallas, Austin, San Antonio, and Houston.

In the fall of 1982, I called him, told him about my plans for Maverick Books, and asked what it would take to buy the rights to *Through Time and the Valley*. I expected him to drive a hard bargain, but he turned out to be a generous man. He offered to sell me his inventory at cost and give me all rights to the book. He wished me the best and told me to call him any time I needed help.

I'll always remember something he told me after we had talked about the difficulties of starting a small business: "If things get bad enough, I'll go back to driving a bulldozer. That's how I worked my way through A&M." That impressed me. I had never known anyone in the literary world who knew how to drive a bulldozer or would have considered doing it.

Over the years, I had the pleasure of meeting him twice, this tall man with sparkling blue eyes, an easy smile, a generous heart, and a firm handshake. I had the highest respect for Bill Shearer and everything he did, and grieved when, in 1996, he died of a brain tumor at the age of 46. It was a terrible loss.

GARAGE BUSINESS

Over the summer months, I worked on converting the garage behind our house into World Headquarters of Maverick Books. Half of the garage had been framed in years before and used as a little apartment, so I had a heated office where I could make phone calls and fill mail orders and storage space for boxes of books. I built floor-to-ceiling bookshelves on one wall and made a shipping table from an old countertop that had come out of one of my father's rental houses.

The first pallet of *The Devil in Texas* arrived at the freight warehouse on August 27, 1982. I loaded the boxes into the back of my little Datsun pickup and moved them into the garage-office. I stopped doing handyman work and became a full-time author/publisher. I often say that since that day, I've never held an honest job. Sink or swim, I had become an author and publisher.

I continued my pattern of rising between 4:30 and 5:30 and writing for four hours. I was working on novels, newspaper articles, book reviews, and essays, anything that would bring in a paycheck. After my writing time, I turned to the publishing business: filling orders, answering mail, making deposits, writing advertising copy, calling stores, delivering books, and making speaking appearances.

My average workday ranged between fourteen and sixteen hours. Kris and our two children pitched in and worked beside me, often into the night. Maverick Books had become my lifeboat on a stormy sea.

SELLING BOOKS

The northern Panhandle had very few bookstores, so I had to find ways of selling directly to the customers. Since I had done a lot of writing for *Livestock Weekly*, I had reason to suppose that subscribers might recognize my name. I bought ads in *LW* that brought in orders from ranch people who lived outside my immediate area—Oklahoma, Kansas, New Mexico, and distant parts of Texas. Kris and I filled the orders in the garage and usually had them in the mail the day they arrived.

Another method I used was to set up a table in locations where a crowd had already gathered. Instead of trying to draw customers into a bookstore, where I was competing against twenty thousand other books, I tried to sell books to people who were already there. County fairs, rodeos, craft shows, and local celebrations were good settings.

I even tried selling books at livestock auctions, but those venues were a waste of time. Cattle auctions draw a crowd of men, and I soon learned that males involved in agriculture buy horse feed, tools, chewing tobacco, and not much else. They will talk to an author but rarely buy his book. Their wives do all the buying for the household. Go find the wives.

Early on, I figured out that the most effective selling venue for me was one that allowed me to read my stories aloud to an audience, taking advantage of a feature that was unique to my stories: They were meant to be read aloud. I discovered that I had enough acting skills to do an effective job as a performer. After the performance, I sold books.

It was a slow but honest way to build an audience.

CHAPTER 30

FINDING HANK*

Most of the literary fame I have acquired in my lifetime has come through my association with Hank the Cowdog, so it would be appropriate to close with a glimpse of how that circumstance occurred.

I wish I could say that I planned Hank's appearance in the literary world and predicted that he would become a star, but that's not the way it happened. I wasn't looking for Hank. We just found each other after I'd been writing every day for fourteen years.

My memory of that period is a bit hazy. It happened long ago, during a time when I was scrambling to make a living and giving no thought to recording historical details. Let's see . . .

I wrote "Confessions of a Cowdog" in January 1981.

The story ran in *The Cattleman* magazine several

*Portions of this chapter appeared in *Finding Hank* (Maverick Books, 2019).

months later.

In the winter of 1982, I made the decision to start Maverick Books and self-publish *The Devil in Texas*.

"Confessions of a Cowdog" was one of the fourteen stories in that book.*

By the summer of 1982, I was looking for opportunities to publicize my new publishing venture and drum up future sales. Our town had a number of groups and civic clubs that held weekly or monthly meetings and were always looking for someone to do a free program.

I was happy to volunteer. In my programs, I talked about my experiences as an author (I was the only one in town), then read one or two of my stories aloud.

My father was a member of the Rotary Club, and it didn't take him long to get me invited to do a program at their weekly meeting. At that time, my favorite read-aloud stories from *The Devil in Texas* were "The World's First Cowboy" and "Diary of a Bronc." But at the Rotary meeting, I decided to read "Confessions of a Cowdog." I had never tried it on an audience and wanted to see how the Rotarians would respond.

I was shocked. They roared with laughter, and I thought we might have to administer oxygen to the town's optometrist, Dr. Billy Nowlin. He was laughing so hard he almost fell out of his chair. After the program, he came loping up to me. "Johnny, that was great! You've got to do more with that dog!" He was the only person in town who called me "Johnny."

It's hard to calculate the importance of his response, because up until that moment, I had never suspected that there was

* In spring 2024, Maverick Books brought out a new edition of *The Devil in Texas* but with a new and more appropriate title: *Confessions of a Cowdog and Other Cowboy Stories*.

magic in those characters. To me, it was just one of fourteen yarns I had dashed off over a three-week period—funny but not anything special.

FROM SHORT STORY TO NOVEL

Now the thought occurred to me . . . maybe I should give the dog a whole book, a novel. Could I make the jump from a seven-page short story to a novel? I wasn't sure I had that much interest in the characters or that I could sustain the energy in a longer story, but around the first of June 1982, I gave it a try.

I got off to a blazing start and dashed off three chapters in three days, but there the story came to a halt. I didn't know where to go and didn't have time to mess with it. I stayed busy over the summer, writing twelve articles for *Equus* magazine, doing two articles for *Texas Highways*, and working on several historical novels.

I didn't get back to the Hank book until the fall and still wasn't sure what to do with it. I thought the first three chapters were pretty good, but I wanted to test them out on a friendly audience.

I chose Tom Ellzey, my old cowboy companion, and drove down to the ranch on Wolf Creek. I had been employed on the LZ Ranch when I wrote the original Hank short story, and that is the ranch I have in mind today when I write a Hank story. In the early books, the character of High Loper was modeled more or less on Tom, and Slim Chance more or less on me.

Tom and I sat in his living room, and I read my three chapters, doing the voices of Hank, Drover, Slim, Loper, and Pete the Barncat. Tom laughed until tears rolled down his cheeks, and when I was done, he roared, "Erickson, you've got to finish that book!"

Tom was hardly an impartial judge, but his response was so enthusiastic, the next morning I went to my writing office, determined to push the story out of the ditch and keep it moving. Four hours later, I had written chapter 4, "The Boxer." It contained the now-famous scene where little Drover asks a ferocious boxer dog, "What would you do if we peed on your tires?"

Once I had gotten the story moving again, the writing must have come without effort, because there was no mention of it in my journal until October 8, when I made an astonishingly casual entry: "I have finished *Hank the Cowdog and the Chicken House Murders*. Ready to send it to the typesetter."

It is worth noting that all the major characters that appeared later in the series of books were present, fully formed, in the first story that appeared in *The Cattleman*: Hank, Drover, Pete, Slim, High Loper, and Sally May.

"I DON'T WRITE FOR CHILDREN!"

Kris served as my editor and made the casual observation that it would make a good children's book, to which I snarled, "It's not a children's book! I don't write for children."

I knew nothing about children's literature and still don't. The reader I had in mind was someone like myself, a slow-reading adult with a lively sense of humor who spent most of his time outside, working with livestock. If I had been writing for children, I would have written *down* to what I perceived to be a child's level and would have greatly underestimated children's ability to comprehend the subtilties and nuances of humor.

I find it interesting that Livy Clemens, Mark Twain's wife, gave the same response when she read *Tom Sawyer* in manuscript. She said it was a book for boys. In a letter to a friend, Twain fumed, "It is *not* a boy's book, at all. It will only be read by adults. It is only written for adults." Several months later, he wrote to the same friend, saying that he had come to agree with Livy: it was a book for boys.

As usual, Kris's instincts were right on target. Although my original audience consisted of adults involved in agriculture, the circle began to widen, and children started reading the books. It was a natural phenomenon that happened on its own, without any scheming or advertising. Teachers were quick to notice that kids were reading Hank books at recess, and I started getting calls to do school programs.

By the fall of 1982, Maverick Books was rolling. I had sold 1,200 copies of *The Devil in Texas* in a little more than a month, had ordered a second printing, and had decided to bring out the new Hank book in the spring. Those were busy times, and the Hank book received no coddling. Kris proofed the manuscript and suggested changes, I made the revisions, and we sent it to Tom Sheahan, the typesetter in Omaha.

Sheahan suggested that we drop "The Chicken House Murders" from the title. He thought it sounded too harsh. I didn't agree but followed his advice.

I've made a lot of mistakes over the years, but I give myself credit for paying attention to what Billy Nowlin (and, later, others in the community) told me: "You need to do more with that dog!" They saw magic in the Hank stories, and I was blind to it. I shiver at the thought of what might have happened if . . .

I hadn't done that program for the Rotarians.
I'd read a different story.
Billy Nowlin hadn't been there.
Billy had been there but hadn't told me it was special.
He'd told me and I hadn't listened.

Sometimes blessings come disguised as dumb luck.

A LITERARY VEHICLE

Before Hank came along, I had spent years trying to tell stories in voices that were grammatical, educated, sophisticated, and literary, but those attempts didn't turn out well. I wrote the first Hank book in a voice that fitted me like an old pair of boots. I was entirely at ease, telling a story in the voice of a ranch dog who had delusions of grandeur and wasn't very smart.

I didn't use an outline and never knew, from one day to the next, where the story was going. At the end, it had a structure that resembled the architecture of a song. It began with an opening statement (a G chord), built tension (a C chord), built more tension (a D chord), and resolved back into G.

That became the template for all the books in the series and gave me a literary vehicle that expressed structure and meaning, in an environment of innocent, organic humor. In other words, it wasn't just another literary howl about absurd creatures inhabiting an absurd universe.

Hank is a fool and a sinner, but he's not absurd. The world he inhabits as Head of Ranch Security throbs with meaning, but with an odd twist. The events he describes are not the same ones we perceive as outside observers. Between those two poles of perception, humor leaps like an arc of electricity.

There is a timeless quality in the Hank stories that offers some immunity to the convulsions of American popular culture: ideology, fashion, sociology, and politics. The stories have even overcome the taint of "regionalism," the term I heard so often during my apprentice years. Dogs aren't regional. They have shared the lives and porches of human beings for at least ten thousand years, and people in China and Iran laugh just as often and just as hard at their dogs as we do in Texas.

Because I'm a slow reader, I tailored the stories to accommodate slow readers. I wanted a Hank story to be fast, pleasant, exciting, and funny. I wanted that slow-reading kid in the fourth grade to laugh out loud, fly through the story, and finish in a moment of triumph: "Hey, Mom, I read a whole book!"

I use short paragraphs and short sentences, and I try to make the prose simple and clear, the kind of sentences that can be diagrammed: subject/verb/object. Each book has twelve chapters, and I limit each chapter to seven double-spaced pages, which I judge to be the attention span of the average rancher, cowboy, fourth-grade boy—and me.

One of the unanticipated results of using this template is that I receive a number of letters from parents and teachers of children who are autistic, dyslexic, or just don't enjoy reading. They will read Hank books when they can't or won't read anything else.

HANK'S WORLD

The literary device of describing the world through the eyes and voice of a dog has given me tremendous artistic freedom. Hank's mind wanders. He loses track of what he's talking about. He misuses language and is a fountain of malapropisms. He exaggerates and winds himself up in a web of silly lies to cover his mistakes—something that children find very funny, since they do it all the time.

Hank describes things he doesn't understand. When he is terrified by the appearance of a one-eyed robot monster, we understand that he is seeing Slim Chance in a welder's hood. When he tells about his encounter with the Silver Monster Bird, he is deadly serious, but we know that he has been barking at a low-flying airplane.

Some of the funniest passages occur when Hank and Drover are awakened in the middle of the night. Half-asleep, they carry on an incoherent conversation, babbling like lunatics—exactly the way my dogs on the porch would talk if we could comprehend them. I sometimes feel guilty that I have been given the opportunity to write entire pages of English prose that don't make a bit of sense. They don't make sense, but they're funny.

FINAL THOUGHTS

I have been working on this infernal book for fifteen years, trying to understand how all this came to pass. I've given it my best effort, but it remains implausible and mysterious—that a small-town kid aspired to be Hemingway, moved far away, failed, and ended up back home, working for a dog—the best job I can imagine.

The Hank stories have given me a medium for writing exactly the kind of stories I wanted to write, which is every author's dream. Self-publishing gave me the freedom to experiment and develop my artistic vision, then to protect it from the coarsening influences of consumerism and popular culture. If my parents were still alive, I think they would be proud. I know they would.

I'm writing this in July 2023. Last February, Mark Erickson and I met at the Audio Refinery in Amarillo to record two songs for the next Hank audiobook, #79 in the series. (By odd coincidence, Kris and I are both 79 years old.) Mark played guitar and bass. With arthritic fingers, I added a few licks on my Stelling banjo and Erik Chapman laid down a track on violin. Erik was raised in Amarillo, attended the Juilliard School, and now plays with the London Philharmonic Orchestra.

Nikki Earley was finishing up her illustrations for the next Hank book. Gary Rinker, my business partner, and his wife Kim were at the Maverick Books warehouse in Perryton, putting UPS stickers on boxes of Hank books bound for Ingram, the big wholesaler in Nashville. From there, they will go to Amazon, Barnes & Noble, Christianbooks.com, and independent bookstores. Every book those companies sell originated in my hometown.

In the fall of 1983, my brother Charles was visiting us in Perryton and had just read the second Hank book, *The Further Adventures*. He was a very perceptive fellow and recognized something special in the story. He asked, "How would you feel if you were remembered as the author of Hank the Cowdog?"

I hadn't quite given up on being Hemingway and snapped, "I wouldn't like it at all!"

Ah well. One remembers the line from a Garth Brooks song, which he probably cribbed from the Bible: "Some of God's greatest gifts are unanswered prayers."

REFERENCES

Bennett, William J. *The Devaluing of America: The Fight for Our Culture and Our Children.* Summit Books, 1992.

Dobie, Frank, and Jeff C. Dykes. *44 Range Country Books Topped Out by J. Frank Dobie in 1941 and 44 More Range Country Books Topped Out by Jeff Dykes in 1971.* Encino Press, 1972.

Erickson, John R. *Finding Hank: The Most-Often Asked Questions About Hank the Cowdog.* Maverick Books, 2019.

———. *Panhandle Cowboy.* University of Nebraska Press, 1980.

———. *Prairie Gothic: The Story of a West Texas Family.* University of North Texas Press, 2005.

———. *Story Craft: Reflections on Faith, Culture, and Writing from the Author of Hank the Cowdog.* Maverick Books, 2009.

Foster-Harris, William. *The Basic Formulas of Fiction.* University of Oklahoma Press, 1944.

Graves, John. *Goodbye to a River.* Alfred A. Knopf, 1960.

———. *The John Graves Reader.* Austin: University of Texas Press, 1996.

———. *Myself and Strangers: A Memoir of Apprenticeship.* Alfred A. Knopf, 2004.

Greene, A. C. *The Fifty Best Books on Texas.* Pressworks

Publishing, 1982.

Guinness, Os. *The Dust of Death: The Sixties Counterculture and How It Changed America Forever*. Crossway Books, 1994.

———. *Time for Truth*. Baker Books, 2007.

Gwynne, S. C. *Empire of the Summer Moon*. Scribner, 2010.

Haley, J. Evetts. *Charles Goodnight: Cowman and Plainsman*. University of Oklahoma Press, 1949.

Kelton, Elmer. *Elmer Kelton Country: The Short Nonfiction of a Texas Novelist*. TCU Press, 1993.

———. *The Time It Never Rained*. TCU Press, 1984.

L'Amour, Louis. *Education of a Wandering Man*. Bantam Books, 1990.

McGrath, Alister E. *The Intellectual World of C. S. Lewis*. Wiley-Blackwell, 2014.

McMahon, Thomas. *Principles of American Nuclear Chemistry: A Novel*. Little Brown and Co., 1970.

McMurtry, Larry. *Film Flam: Essays on Hollywood*. Touchstone, 1987.

———. *In a Narrow Grave: Essays on Texas*. University of New Mexico Press, 1968.

———. *Literary Life: A Second Memoir*. Simon & Schuster, 2009.

———. *Walter Benjamin at the Dairy Queen: Reflections at Sixty and Beyond*. Simon & Schuster, 1999.

Medved, Michael. *Right Turns: From Liberal Activist to Conservative Champion in 35 Unconventional Lessons*. Three Rivers Press, 2004.

Silber, John. *Straight Shooting: What's Wrong with America and How to Fix It*. Harper & Row, 1989.

Wouk, Herman. *The Language God Talks: On Science and Religion*. Little, Brown and Company, 2010.

———. *This Is My God*. Little, Brown and Company, 1987.

———. *The Will to Live On: This Is Our Heritage*. Cliff Street Books, 2000.

INDEX

activism, 18, 47–48, 71–72. *See also* Civil Rights Movement
Adam, Adam (Erickson), 28–31
Adventures of Bookie Tanner (Erickson), 114–15
advertising, 262–63
airplane trips, 137–41
alcohol, 11–12, 23–24, 118–21
"Alkali County Tales" (Erickson), 217–18
Altizer, Thomas J. J., 63
American Cowboy, 179
antiwar movement, 46–48, 58
Applebaum, Irwyn, 203, 242–43, 250
articles, written by Erickson
- for *Dallas Morning News*, 242
- as fiction, 218, 240
- on fires, 179
- humorous, 270–72 (*see also* short stories, humorous, Erickson's)
- for ranching journals/magazines, 164, 201, 217, 225, 267

atheism/atheists, 7–8, 57–60
audiobooks, 272
Austin (TX). *See* St. Johns community (TX)

Bad Smoke, Good Smoke: A Texas Rancher's View of Wildfire (Erickson), 179
Baptists vs. Catholics, 62–63
Barnett, Ross, 75–76, 79
bartender Larry, 128–30
Basic Formulas of Fiction (Foster-Harris), 154
Beasley, John, 246–48
Bible, first sentence of, 55, 183
Bill (college friend), 11–12
Bill (the cook), 131–32
Black, Baxter, 254–56
Black population. *See* St. Johns community (TX)
Blanton, Judy, 8–9
Boller, Paul F., 12–13
Bone Pickers, The (Dewlen), 151, 155
books, value of, 196
book sales, 262–63
Brooklyn Protestant Parish, 79–81
brothels, 140–41

Campbell, Walter Stanley, 153
Canadian River Valley, 173–74. *See also Through Time and the Valley* (Erickson)
Carne-Ross, Donald, 14
carpentry, 241

Carter, Hodding, 74
cartoons, self-published, 253–54
Casey the bronc, 230–31, 233–39
Catcher in the Rye, The (Salinger), 7
Catholics vs. Baptists, 62–63
cattle-feeding industry, 137–41
Cattleman, The, 164, 217, 229, 240, 242
chaplain assistant, Erickson as, 43–44
Chapman, Erik, 272
character, determination of, 207
character sketches
  about, 122–23
  of country club cowboys, 125–26
  of Larry the bartender, 128–30
  of Mrs. Farnsworth, 127–28
  of Mrs. Wells, 126–27
  of Old Bill, the cook, 131–32
  of Sherry, the cocktail waitress, 132–35
Charles Goodnight: Cowman and Plainsman (Haley), 39–41. *See also* Goodnight, Charles
Charlie Goodnight: His Life in Poetry and Song (Wilkinson), 167–70. *See also* Goodnight, Charles
chess, 138
children's books, 268–69
choirs, 16–17
Christianity. *See also* religion
  Catholics vs. Baptists, 62–63
  on enslavement, 58–59
  in Erickson's writing, 231
  faith, defense of, 57–60, 70
  God is Dead theology, 63
  of Joe Erickson, 225
  vs. Nietzsche, 58–60
  on war, 58
Civil Rights Movement
  Brooklyn volunteerism and, 79–81
  Evers and, 75–79
  Mississippi racial study and, 72–77
  in New York City, 77–81
  race relations ministry and, 83–86, 90–92, 99
  racial issues, early thought on, 69–70
  in St. Johns community (TX) (*see* St. Johns community (TX))
  violence and, 78–79
Clemmons, Olin, 27
College House, at University of Texas (Austin), 25–26
college years
  activism during, 18, 47–48
  Civil Rights Movement work during (*see* Civil Rights Movement)
  classes of, 9–10, 12–14, 17–18, 43–44, 52–53
  dating in, 12
  end of, 61–62, 64–65, 97–98
  friends during, 7–8, 10–12, 27, 30, 72, 77
  at Harvard Divinity School/Harvard College (*see* Harvard Divinity School/Harvard College)
  jobs during, 18, 43–44, 56–57
  mental health in, 10–12
  national climate during, 21–24, 65, 71
  religious thought during, 7–8, 22, 37–38, 57–60
  student type, Erickson's, 9, 38
  at University of Denver, 6–8
  at University of Texas (Austin) (*see* University of Texas (Austin))
Collins, John, 77–78
Comanches, 39–41
Communion (Strieber), 19
"Confessions of a Cowdog" (Erickson), 239, 266–67. *See also* Hank the Cowdog stories
conventions, Western Writers of America (WWA), 199–204, 248–51

cook, Bill, 131–32
counseling, 10–11
Count of Monte Cristo, The (Dumas), 147
Cowboy County (Erickson), 224
cowboy years
  challenges of, 221–22
  at Crown Ranch, 177, 215–17
  economic return and, 221
  father's concerns regarding, 222–26
  as inspiration for writings, 191, 215–17, 228–31, 267
  livestock publication writing and (*see under* articles, written by Erickson)
  at LZ Ranch, 222, 267
cowboys, character sketches of, 125–26
Cowpokes cartoon, 253–54
Cox, Harvey, 48
Crown Ranch (Beaver County, OK), 177, 215–17
culture, Texas, 170
Curry, Mabel Sherman (grandmother), 39

dance drama, for Kris, 28–31
dancing, 89
deaths. *See* murders
Decon, Ellen, 29–31
depression. *See* mental health
Devil in Texas, The (Erickson), 261–62, 269
Dewlen, Al, 151–55
"Diary of a Bronc" (Erickson), 230–31, 233–39, 256
dishonesty, 206
Dobie, J. Frank, 147–48, 158, 160

East Harlem Protestant Parish, 77–78
editors, merit of, 250–51
Edstrom, Mickey, 7–8
education
  classroom vs life experiences, 112–14, 176–77
  discrimination of those without, 110, 112
  of Erickson (*see* college years)
Ellis, Carl, 104–5
Ellzey, Bill, 173, 191
Ellzey, Lawrie, 30
Ellzey, Tom, 230, 267–68
Empire of the Summer Moon (Gwynne), 40
enslavement, Christian thought on, 58–59
Epic of Gilgamesh, 115
Erickson, Anna Beth (Curry) (mother), 29, 100–101, 223
Erickson, Charles (brother), 8, 71–72
Erickson, John R.
  award presented to, 179
  cowboy years of (*see* cowboy years)
  economic conditions of, 51, 154, 221–22, 246, 258–59
  education of, college years (*see* college years)
  education of, high school, 5–6, 16
  faith of (*see* Christianity; religion)
  family of (*see* family, of Erickson)
  father, relationship with, 31, 102, 106–7, 222–26
  friends of (*see* friends, of Erickson)
  homes of (*see* homes, Ericksons')
  humbling of, post college, 112–14, 120–21
  jobs of (*see* jobs, Erickson's)
  letter exchanges (*see* letter exchanges)
  mental health of, 10–12
  morals of, 56–57, 140–41 (*see also* religion)
  music and (*see* music)
  publishing company of (*see* Maverick Books)
  racial relations and, 83–86,

90–92 (*see also* Civil Rights Movement)
regional identity of, 148
wife of (*see* Erickson, Kristine (Dykema) (wife))
writings by (*see* writings, by Erickson)
Erickson, Joseph (father)
about, 28, 100–102, 105–6
assistance from, to son, 222, 259–60
concern for son by, 222–26
courtship and wedding of, 101
faith of, 225
generosity of, 259–60
jobs of, 100, 102, 104–5
John, relationship with, 31, 102, 106–7
opinion of son, 223–25
Erickson, Kristine (Dykema) (wife)
character of, 27–28
courting of, 27–28, 49
dance drama for, 28–31
Maverick Books and, 257–58
meeting of, 20, 26–27
proposal and marriage of, 49–50
support of writing from, 51–52
Erickson, Mark (son), 194, 272
Evers, Medgar, 75–79

failure, feelings of, 243–44
faith. *See* Christianity; religion
family, of Erickson
Aunt Ada, 102–3
Charles (brother), 8, 71–72
father (*see* Erickson, Joseph (father))
grandmother, 39
Martha Sherman (great-great-grandmother), 40–41
Mike Harter (cousin), 62–63
mother, 29, 100–101, 223
son, 194, 272
wife (*see* Erickson, Kristine (Dykema) (wife))
farmhand, work as, 110–12
Farnsworth, Mrs., 127–28
father-son relationship, of John and Joe, 31, 102, 106–7, 222–26
Ferguson, Wendell, 110–12
fiction, in magazines, 218, 240
fires
documents destroyed by, 2017, 186–87, 198
Panhandle, 2006, 178–79
football, in St. Johns community (TX), 86–88
40 Years' Gatherin's (Van Cleve), 201
Foster Harris, William "Foster-Harris," 153–55
Friedman, Alan, 13, 17
Friedman, Richard "Kinky," 21
friends, of Erickson
in college years, 7–8, 10–12, 27, 30, 72, 77
interracial, 72, 88–90
professional, 177–78, 186, 191, 206–7, 248, 250
at University of Denver, 72
From a Limestone Ledge (Graves), 176

gentrification, 84–86
Gnostic Gospels (Pagels), 42
God is Dead theology, 63
Goetzmann, William H., 18
Gone with the Wind (Mitchell), 146–47
Good, Keith, 258–59
Good Old Boys, The (Kelton), 208–10
Goodbye to a River: A Narrative (Graves), 171–74
Goodnight, Charles
Haley on, 158, 162–63
impact of, on writers, 163
Sherman death and, 40
Wilkinson on, 167–70
Gordon, Henry, 88–92

Graves, John
  about, 171–73
  death of, 180
  genre of, 171, 173
  on Goodnight, 163
  impact of on Erickson, 173–75
  meeting of, Erickson's, 175
  praise for, 176–77
  as regional writer, 121
  relationship with Erickson, 177–80
  work ethic of, 175–76
  works of, 171–74, 176
Greene, A. C., 159–60, 172
Guggenheim Fellowship, 242
Guinness, Os, 22

Haley, J. Evetts
  about, 158
  controversy and, 159
  Goodnight and, 39, 162–63
  as historian, 159–60
  interview with, 160–62
  legacy of, 163–65
  praise for, 159–60, 163
  as regional writer, 121
  works of, 39–41, 159
Hank the Cowdog stories
  audience of, 270–71
  as children's books, 268–69
  fan praise on, 202
  as fiction, 240
  first appearance of, 231
  Foster-Harris impact on, 154
  genesis of, 265–67
  Hank, about, 271–72
  illustrations for, 257–58
  inspiration for, 216
  as novels, 267–68
  readings of, 197
  structure of, 270–71
  writing of, 239
Hard Scrabble (Graves), 176
Harter, Mike (cousin), 62–63
Harvard Divinity School/ Harvard College
  about, 41–42
  antiwar movement at, 46–48
  application to, 38
  classes at, 43–44, 52–53
  professors at (*see* professors during college years)
  reflection on, 63–65
  small-town kid at, 38, 63–64
  social life during, 49
Hemingway, Ernest, 146–47
"Hero in Literature, The" course, 14
Holmes, Gerald, 256–57
homes, Ericksons'
  in Beaver County (OK), 189, 218
  in Boston, 50–51
  in Perryton, 109, 222
  in St. Johns community (TX), 84–85
honesty, 206–7
Horn, Paul, 217–18
horse breaking, 230–31
Horseman, Pass By (McMurtry), 154–55
house restoration, 246–48
humor writing, 217–18, 229–31, 256, 270–72
Hunter, The (Erickson), 115

infidelity, 56–57
intelligence, lesson on, 112
Intercollegiate Socialist Society, 44
interracial ministries. *See also* Civil Rights Movement
  Ministry Among Neighbors, 83–86, 99
  Operation Brotherhood, 90–92
Isaacs, Lee "Lee-Lee," 88
Iscoe, Ira, 12

jealousy, among writers, 198

jobs, Erickson's
carpenter's helper, 241
in cattle-feeding industry, 137–41
during college, 18, 43–44, 56–57
as cowboy (*see* cowboy years)
farmhand, 110–12
handyman, self-employed, 245–48
Perryton Club, 118, 120–23
publisher (*see* Maverick Books)
Jones, Tommy Lee, 209–10
Journey Song (Erickson), 185–87
Judaism, 182–84
Just War Doctrine, 58

Kelton, Elmer
about, 205
as American novelist, 207–8
commonalities of, with Erickson, 205–6
correspondence, Erickson's with, 206–7
editing of *Journey Song* by, 186
on Goodnight, 163
honesty of, 206
literary fame of, 210–11
works of, 157–58, 208–10
King, Martin Luther, Jr., 83
Kiowa people, 185
Klein, Michael, 7
Knighton, Jeff, 241–44

L'Amour, Louis, 201–4, 227
Language God, The (Wouk), 184
Larry the bartender, 128–30
Last Picture Show, The (McMurtry), 193
letter exchanges, with professionals
Graves, 178–80
Haley, 164
Kelton, 206–7, 209
McMurtry, 192
Silber, 16
Wouk, 183–85
Lewis, C. S., 60, 70
liberalism, 72
liquor. *See* alcohol
Livestock Weekly, 164, 201, 211, 217, 262
"Leg of a Cow Horse" (Erickson), 239
Lonely Crowd, The (Riesman), 44
Lonely Mad Artists (Students for a Democratic Society), 23
Lonesome Dove (McMurtry), 193–94
LZ Ranch, 222, 239, 267

magazines, articles for. *See* articles, written by Erickson
Maverick Books
contributors to, 256–57
financing for, 258–60
genesis of, 244, 256–58, 261–62
marketing and, 262–63
Mbawa, Naboth, 77, 83–84
McLain, Dean, 118
McMahon, Tom, 53–55
McMurtry, Larry
correspondence, Erickson's with, 192
Dewlen on, 154–55
Erickson on, 193–94
on Haley, 159–60
meeting of, Erickson's, 196–98
presentation by, 197
on West and Western lifestyle, 193–96
works of, 154–55, 191, 193–95
mental health
of Erickson in college, 10–12
of intellects, 89–90
of writers, 23, 54–55
Mexico, travel to, 139–41
Millsaps College, 74
ministries, interracial, 83–86, 90–92, 99. *See also* St. Johns community (TX)
Ministry Among

Neighbors, 83–86, 99
miracles, 59
Mississippi, racial study in, 72–77
morality, 206
Morrison, Theodore, 52–53
movies, books made into
Good Old Boys, The (Kelton), 209
by McMurtry, 191, 193–94
Twilight of Honor (Kelton), 209–10
murders
during Civil Rights Movement, 74, 78–79
by Native Americans, 39–41
at University of Texas (Austin), 35–36
music
choirs, 16–17
dance drama and, 28–31
in Hang the Cowdog stories, 257, 272
rebellious, 71
tastes in, Erickson's, 50
Texas, 168–70
of Wilkinson on Goodnight, 167–70
Myself and Strangers (Graves), 172–73

national climate, of 1960s, 21–24, 65, 71
Native Americans, 39–41, 185
New York City, racial work in, 77–81
Nietzsche, Friedrich, 57–60
1960s, 21–24, 54, 65. *See also* college years
novels
attempts at, Erickson's, 110, 217–18, 228–29, 242–43
challenges of, 145–46
as dark, in 1960s, 54
Dewlen and, 151, 154–55
Erickson's, 114–15, 185–87, 267–68
Kelton and, 157–58, 207–8, 210–11
L'Amour and, 201–3
McMahon's impact regarding, 55
McMurtry and, 154–55, 193
O'Brien and, 248–50
read in college, 7
Wouk and, 181–84

O'Brien, Jerry, 248–51
Operation Brotherhood, 90–92

pacifism, 26, 44–45
Pagels, Elaine, 42–43
Panhandle Cowboy (Erickson), 191–92
Parrish, Clarence, 241
Perryton (TX)
about, 5–8, 103
alcohol prohibition in, 119–20
residents of, character sketches and (*see* character sketches)
Perryton Club, 118–23, 125–35
Pilkington, Tom, 196
place, sense of, 160, 209–10
Plan II (honors program), 9
plays, written by Erickson, 17–18, 28–31
plot maps, 146
poetry, 167–69, 254–56
Pojman, Lou, 80
police, interaction with, 76–77
political correctness, 114–15
poverty, 221. *See also under* Erickson, John R.: economic conditions of
Prairie Gothic (Erickson), 41, 179
Principles of American Nuclear Chemistry: A Novel (McMahon), 55
professors during college years
Boller, 12–13
Carne-Ross, 14
Cox, 48
Friedman, 13, 17
Goetzmann, 18

Harvard Divinity School's top, 42
Iscoe, 12–14
Morrison, Theodore, 52–53
Niebuhr, H. Richard, 43
Riesman, 44–45
Silber, 14–16
Smith, W. C., 43
Stendahl, 43
prohibition, in Texas, 118–21
proposal/wedding, of John and Kris, 49–50
prostitution, 140–41

Quakers (Society of Friends), 26

racial issues, 72–77, 83–86, 91. *See also* Civil Rights Movement
Radical Theology and the Death of God (Altizer), 63
ranch life. *See also* cowboy years
challenges of, 221–22
family history of, Erickson's, 6, 39, 192, 222–23
Haley and, 158, 161
honesty and, 206–7
as inspiration for writing, 191, 215–17, 228–31, 267
Through Time and the Valley and (*see Through Time and the Valley* (Erickson))
rape, 41
reading
as challenging, for Erickson, 9, 146, 268, 270–71
of classics, in college, 7, 13–14
as form of study, 146–47
rebellion, 21–24, 58–60, 71
Reid, Ace, 253–54
rejections, from publishers, 114–15, 174, 186, 219, 228–29, 243–44
religion. *See also* Christianity
in college years, 7–8, 22, 37–38, 57–60
Judaism, 182, 184
rebellion from, 58–60, 71
Wouk and, 182–83
reservations, Native American, 185
Riesman, David, 44–45
Rotary Club reading, 266–67

"Sally May's Journal" (Erickson), 256
Salter, John, 73–75, 79
School of Professional Writing (SPW) at University of Oklahoma, 153–54
school shooting, 33–36
Secular City, The (Cox), 48
segregation, 72–73, 76, 84–86
self-employment, 245–48
self-publishing, 249, 253–56
Seminole (TX), 39
Shakespeare course, 13
Sheahan, Tom, 258, 269
Shearer, Bill, 260–61
Sherman, Martha (great-great-grandmother), 40–41
Sherry, the cocktail waitress, 132–35
Shoal Creek Publishers, 218–20, 260
shooting, at University of Texas (Austin), 33–36
short stories, humorous, Erickson's
"Alkali County Tales," 217–18
"Confessions of a Cowdog," 239 (*see also* Hank the Cowdog stories)
Devil in Texas, 261–62, 269
"Diary of a Bronc," 230–31, 233–39, 256
"Log of a Cow Horse," 239
"Sally May's Journal," 256
"World's First Cowboy, The," 256
Silber, John, 14–16
Simmons, Marc, 189–91
slavery, Christian thought on, 58–59
small-town life
business in, 246, 259

character sketches of (*see* character sketches)
civic clubs in, 266–67
education and, 112
personal exposure in, 224
writers from, 148–49
socialism, 44–46
Society of Friends (Quakers), 26
Southern Baptist Church, on racial issues, 70
SPW (School of Professional Writing) at University of Oklahoma, 153–54
St. Johns community (TX)
friends of Ericksons in, 88–90
inspiration of, for writing, 114–15
leaving, 98–99
men of, 86–88
Operation Brotherhood and, 90–92
segregation of, 84–86
violence in, 92–93
Strieber, Whitley, 19
student senate campaign, 18–21
Students for a Democratic Society, 23

Texan Looks at Lyndon, A (Haley), 159
Theological Education Fund, 38
This Is My God (Wouk), 184
Thomas, Norman, 44–46
Thompson, Luther, 218–19
Through Time and the Valley (Erickson)
Haley on, 164
inspiration for, 121
praise for, 189–90
publishing of, 218–20
research for, 173–74
rights of, bought by Erickson, 260–61
Till, Emmett, 74
Time It Never Rained, The (Kelton), 208
tractor, writing on, 110–11, 115
travel, through Canadian River Valley, 173–74
Twilight of Honor (Dewlen), 151, 154

University of Denver, 6–8
University of Oklahoma, 153–54
University of Texas (Austin)
classes at, 9–10, 12–14, 17–18
Plan II at, 8–9, 17
professors at (*see* professors during college years)
rebellion during, 19, 22–23
shooting at, 33–36
social life during, 7, 10–11, 25–26

Van Cleve, Spike, 200–201
Vestal, Stanley, 153
Vietnam War, 46–48
violence
among Black population, 92–93
during Civil Rights Movement, 74, 78–79

waitress, Sherry, 132–35
Walter Benjamin at the Dairy Queen (McMurtry), 194–95
war, Christian thought on, 58
Wells, Mrs., 126–27
Western Horseman, 217
Western writers. *See* writers, Western
Western Writers of America (WWA) conventions, 199–204, 248–51
White Citizens' Councils, 74–75
Whitman, Charles, 34–36
wildfires. *See* fires
Wilkinson, Andy, 167–70
Wittliff, Bill, 174, 194
"World's First Cowboy, The" (Erickson), 256
Wouk, Herman
about, 182–85
admiration for, Erickson's, 182–83, 185, 187

correspondence with Erickson, 183–85
works of, 181, 184
writers, met by Erickson
Baxter, 255–56
Boller, 13
Dewlen, 151–55
Friedman, R., 21
Goetzmann, 18
Graves, 175 (*see also* Graves, John)
Haley, 160–62 (*see also* Haley, J. Evetts)
Kelton, 205 (*see also* Kelton, Elmer)
McMahon, 53–55
McMurtry, 196–98
Morrison, 52–53
O'Brien, 248
Riesman, 44–45
Simmons, 189–91
Strieber, 19
Van Cleve, 200–201
at Western Writers of American convention, 200
Wittliff, 174
writers, Texan. *See also* writers, Western
Dewlen, 151–55
Foster-Harris, 153–55
Graves (*see* Graves, John)
Haley (*see* Haley, J. Evetts)
McMurtry (*see* McMurtry, Larry)
overview of, 147–49
Wilkinson, 167–70
writers, Western. *See also* writers, Texan
Kelton (*see* Kelton, Elmer)
L'Amour, 201–4
list of, 163
Simmons, 189–91
Wouk (*see* Wouk, Herman)
writing. *See also* writings, by Erickson
challenges of, 112–14, 145–46, 227–30
morning schedule, 51, 112, 118, 121, 176–77
religion and, 182–83
schooling and, 97–98
skills, development of (*see* writing skills development)
sneaking times for, 110–11, 115, 121–23
writing skills development
character sketches and (*see* character sketches)
cowboy work and, 215–17
from Gordon, 90
at Harvard Divinity School/College, 52–53
reading and, 146–47
study of TX authors and, 151–55
at University of Texas (Austin), 17–18
writings, by Erickson
articles (*see* articles, written by Erickson)
character sketches (*see* character sketches)
children's books, 268–69
dance drama, for Kris, 28–31
father's opinion of, 223–24
fiction, articles as, 218, 240
Hank the Cowdog stories (*see* Hank the Cowdog stories)
humorous short stories (*see* short stories, humorous)
humorous short stories, excerpt from, 233–39
nonfiction, 41, 179, 191–92, 224 (*see also Through Time and the Valley* (Erickson))
novels, 114–15, 185–87, 267–68
plays, 17–18, 28–31, 78, 80
rejections of, 114–15, 174, 186, 219, 228–29, 243–44
term paper on Thomas, 44–46

WWA (Western Writers of America) convention, 199–204, 248–51

YMCA, 37–38

youth groups, 77–78, 80, 90–92

Zagmut, Taha, 10

ABOUT THE AUTHOR

John R. Erickson was born in Midland and grew up in Perryton, graduated from the University of Texas, and studied two years at Harvard Divinity School. He is best known for his Hank the Cowdog books. The series has grown to eighty-two volumes that have sold more than 10 million copies. He has been inducted into the Texas Literary Hall of Fame. He has previously published two books with Texas Tech University Press: *Bad Smoke, Good Smoke: A Texas Rancher's View of Wildfire* (2024) and *Porch Talk: A Conversation About Archeology in the Texas Panhandle* (2022). He and his wife Kris have been married since 1967 and live on their ranch in Roberts County.